FROM UNDERDOGS TO CHAMPIONS

THE STORY OF THE EAST TEXAS KINGS
COACH JUSTISS HILL

Publishing Copyright © 2023
Angela Walsh Writing Group

ISBN: 979-8-9866471-5-9

Printed in the United States of America.
All Right Reserved.

Questions or Queries: angelawalshwritinggroup@gmail.com

All rights reserved. Printed in the United States of America. No part of this publication may be reproduced, stored in a retrieval system, or transmitted in any form or by any means electronically, mechanically, photocopying, recording, or otherwise, without the prior written permission of the publisher, except in the case of brief quotations embodied in critical articles and reviews.

Dedication

I want to thank Mr. Joe for always believing in me and always encouraging me to keep pursuing my dreams of becoming a basketball coach. I want to take this time to thank the East Texas Kings basketball program for believing in me, as well, and for allowing me to be the best coach I can be. Thank you Quin Hood for helping me brainstorm for this book. And, last but not least I want to thank Mrs. Angelique Walsh for making this possible

Author
Coach Justiss Hill

From Underdogs To Champions

Table of contents

Dedication		3
Ch. 1	The Birth Of A Dream	9
Ch.2	Building The Foundation	13
Ch.3	The Rise Of The Underdogs	19
Ch.4	Overcoming Adversity	23
Ch.5	The Championship Run	27
Ch. 6	Impact Beyond the Court	31
Ch. 7	Legacy and Future	35
Ch. 8	The Power of Unity	39
Ch. 9	The Heart of a Champion	43
Ch. 10	Celebrating Success	47
Ch. 11	Lessons Learned	51
Ch. 12	Underdogs to Champions	55
Ch. 13	Embracing Change	59
Ch. 14	Sustaining Success	63
Ch. 15	The Power of Mentorship	67
Ch. 16	Facing New Rivals	71
Ch. 17	Balancing Basketball and Academics	75
Ch. 18	The Power of Community Support	79
Ch. 19	Overcoming Self-Doubt	83
Ch. 20	The Evolution of Leadership	87

Ch. 21	The Power of Resilience	91
Ch. 22	Expanding Horizons	95
Ch. 23	Embracing Diversity	99
Ch. 24	The Impact of Coaching	103
Ch. 25	Giving Back To The Community	107
Ch. 26	Navigating Expectations	111
Ch. 27	The Pursuit of Excellence	115
Ch. 28	The Power of Visualization.	119
Ch. 29	Celebrating Individual Achievements	123
Ch. 30	Embracing Adversity	127
Ch. 31	The Spirit of Perseverance	131
Ch. 32	The Impact of Mentorship	135
Ch. 33	Cultivating a Winning Mindset.	139
Ch. 34	The Joy of Teamwork	143
Ch. 35	Leaving a Legacy	147
Ch. 36	The Memorial Service of a Fallen Teammate	151
Ch. 37	Beyond Boundaries	155
Ch. 38	The Heart of Service	159
Ch. 39	Life Lessons from the Game	163
Ch. 40	The Endless Journey	167
Ch. 41	The Spirit of Sportsmanship	169
Ch. 42	Building Bridges Through Basketball	173

Ch. 43	Empowering Women in Sports	177
Ch. 44	The Importance of Mental Health	181
Ch. 45	Mindfulness and Focus	185
Ch. 46	The Impact of Nutrition	189
Ch. 47	Embracing Innovation	193
Ch. 48	Paying Gratitude Forward	197
Ch. 49	Celebrating Diversity and Inclusion	201
Ch. 50	The Power of Endurance	205
Ch. 51	Building Strong Foundations	209
Ch. 52	The Beauty of Team Dynamics	213
Ch. 53	Learning from Legends	217
	About the Author	219
	Team Pictures	220

From Underdogs To Champions

Chapter One: The Birth of a Dream

Once upon a time, in the heart of East Texas, there existed a small and struggling basketball program known as the East Texas Kings. Their team was made up of passionate and dedicated players, but they lacked the resources and recognition to compete at the highest level. For years, they were considered underdogs, often overlooked and underestimated by their competitors.

The East Texas Kings Basketball Program, LLC was founded by Coach Justiss Hill, a former college basketball player with a vision to transform the lives of young athletes through the sport he loved. Despite facing numerous challenges, Coach Hill was determined to turn the program into something special.

In the early days, the Kings faced a lack of funding, outdated training facilities, and a dearth of talented players willing to join a relatively unknown team. However, Coach Hills' unwavering commitment and belief in his players inspired them to work harder than ever before.

The turning point came when a local business owner, Mr. Johnson, noticed the team's dedication and potential during a community basketball tournament. Impressed by their passion and teamwork, he decided to invest in the East Texas Kings, providing them with much-needed financial support. With this newfound backing, the team was able to renovate their facilities, hire experienced coaches, and even offer scholarships to promising young athletes in the region.

Under Coach Hill's guidance and the mentorship of skilled coaches, the Kings began to flourish. They underwent rigorous training, both on and off the court, focusing not just on basketball skills but also on academic excellence and personal development. The players learned the value of discipline, perseverance, and the importance of supporting each other as a family. In their first season with improved resources, the Kings showed remarkable progress. While they didn't win every game, they proved to be formidable opponents, often taking stronger teams to the edge. Their efforts caught the attention of college recruiters, and some of the Kings' players received offers from prestigious basketball programs, earning scholarships to further their education and basketball careers.

With each passing season, the East Texas Kings continued to grow stronger. More talented athletes from across the state sought to join the program, and the team's reputation spread beyond Texas. The community rallied behind them, turning their games into major events, filled with excitement and pride.

After a few years of hard work and dedication, the East Texas Kings found themselves in the state championships, facing off against one of the most dominant teams in Texas. It was a David versus Goliath scenario, but the Kings were no longer the timid underdogs they once were. They had transformed into a team of skilled and fearless champions.

In a thrilling and nail-biting game, the Kings played their hearts out, leaving everything on the court. With seconds left on the clock, the score was tied, and the outcome was uncertain. In a last-minute play, one of the Kings' star players scored a buzzer-beating shot, securing a historic victory for the team.

The East Texas Kings had done the unthinkable - they had gone from underdogs to champions. The whole community erupted in joy and celebration, proud of their team's incredible journey. The news of their triumph spread like wildfire, and the Kings became an inspiration to aspiring athletes everywhere.

As the years went by, the East Texas Kings Basketball Program, LLC continued to thrive, producing numerous college and professional basketball players. But beyond the wins and accolades, the real success of the program lay in the positive impact it had on the lives of its players. The program had given hope and direction to young individuals who might have otherwise been overlooked, transforming them into confident and successful young adults.

And so, the story of the East Texas Kings Basketball Program LLC serves as a timeless reminder that with determination, belief, and the support of a community, even the most unlikely underdogs can rise to become true champions in every sense of the word.

Chapter Two: Building the Foundation

In the quaint town of Naples, nestled deep within the heart of East Texas, a young man named Justiss Hill had always felt a deep connection to basketball. From a tender age, he would spend countless hours dribbling a worn-out basketball on the cracked concrete courts of the local park. His eyes would light up with excitement as he watched college and NBA games on the old television set with his father. Basketball was more than just a sport for Justiss it was his passion, his escape, and his dream.

As he grew older, Justiss' skills on the court began to catch the attention of friends and family. Encouraged by their praise, he dedicated himself to honing his abilities day in and day out. Justiss' dreams reached new heights when he earned a scholarship to play college basketball. He became a standout player on the team, and his natural leadership and talent made him a beloved figure both on and off the court.

During his college years, Justiss met Coach Johnson, a wise and experienced mentor who had led his team to national championships in the past. Coach Philly recognized something special in Justiss – not just his basketball prowess, but his ability to inspire and uplift his teammates. Under Coach Johnson's guidance, Justiss' passion for basketball evolved into a profound desire to help others, to give back to his community, and to make a difference in the lives of young athletes.

Upon graduating from college, Justiss returned to Naples with a burning vision in his heart. He wanted to create a basketball program that would not only produce talented players but also instill values of discipline, teamwork, and perseverance. He dreamed of providing opportunities for kids from all backgrounds – a place where their potential could flourish, regardless of their financial situation.

With an unwavering belief in his dream, Justiss set out on a journey to bring his vision to life. He reached out to local community centers, schools, and youth clubs, sharing his ideas and seeking support for his endeavor. However, the road was far from smooth. Many doubted the feasibility of such a program, while others questioned whether a small town like Naples could ever produce competitive basketball talent.

Undeterred, Justiss continued to advocate for his dream, and his perseverance soon bore fruit. A local business owner named Mr. Johnson, who had watched Justiss' basketball journey from the beginning, saw the passion and potential in the young man's eyes. Mr Philly had always been an avid supporter of youth development in Naples, Texas, and he recognized that Justiss' dream aligned perfectly with his own values.

Together, they decided to establish the East Texas Kings Basketball Program LLC. With Mr. Lamar Philly's financial backing and Justiss' basketball expertise, they began building the foundation of a program that would change lives.

Their first challenge was finding a suitable location for the program. They scouted the town for facilities and eventually came across an abandoned warehouse on the outskirts of Naples, Texas . With Mr. Lamar Philly's assistance, they acquired the space and began transforming it into a state-of-the-art training center.

Over the next few months, Justiss worked tirelessly, organizing tryouts, recruiting talented coaches, and creating a curriculum that focused not just on basketball skills but also on education and personal development. The program's philosophy emphasized the importance of academic excellence, discipline, and community involvement.

Word about the East Texas Kings Basketball Program, LLC began to spread like wildfire through Naples, Texas and neighboring towns. Parents and young athletes were intrigued by the program's vision and commitment to helping children reach their potential both on and off the court. Soon, the program's registration was overflowing with enthusiastic participants.

As the opening day approached, Justiss stood in front of the renovated warehouse, now proudly displaying the East Texas Kings logo. He couldn't help but feel a mix of excitement and nervousness. Would his dream take flight, or would it remain a distant hope?

Little did he know that the birth of the East Texas Kings Basketball Program, LLC was just the beginning of an extraordinary journey. The impact of his dream would reach far beyond anything he could have imagined, touching the lives of countless young athletes and transforming them from ordinary individuals into the Kings of their own destinies.

From Underdogs To Champions

Chapter Three: The Rise of the Underdogs

As the East Texas Kings Basketball Program, LLC continued to grow and flourish, the team's reputation as underdogs gradually started to change. What was once a small and unknown program had transformed into a force to be reckoned within the basketball community.

The Kings' rise to prominence was not without its fair share of challenges. As they entered more competitive tournaments and faced stronger opponents, they encountered setbacks and losses that tested their resilience. But each defeat only fueled their determination to improve and prove their worth on the court.

Coach Justiss Hill and his coaching staff knew that their players had the talent and potential to compete with the best, but they needed to develop mental toughness and strategic acumen. The team devoted countless hours to studying game footage, analyzing opponents' playing styles, and refining their own strategies.

The turning point in their journey came during the regional championships. The Kings faced a formidable opponent in the finals – a team with a long history of dominance in the region. The odds were stacked against them, and many expected the Kings to succumb to the pressure of the big stage.

But, the Kings had other plans. They approached the game with a newfound sense of confidence and determination. Their hard work and dedication had built a strong foundation, and now it was time to showcase their progress.

The championship game was a thrilling display of skill and teamwork. The Kings played with heart and intensity, leaving everything on the court. In a nail-biting finish, they emerged victorious, stunning both the basketball community and themselves. They had defeated the giants and claimed the regional championship – a true underdog story in the making.

The news of the Kings' triumph spread like wildfire, reaching far beyond East Texas. Sports journalists hailed them as the "Cinderella story" of the season, capturing the hearts of basketball fans across the nation. The Kings had become the darlings of the underdog world, inspiring countless young athletes who dreamed of overcoming the odds.

With their newfound success, college recruiters flocked to their games, eager to offer scholarships to the talented players who had proven their mettle on the court. The Kings had become a pathway for young athletes to achieve their dreams of playing college basketball.

However, Coach Justiss and his team remained grounded amidst the newfound fame. They knew that success was not a destination but a journey, and they continued to emphasize the values of hard work, humility, and teamwork to their players.

As the years went by, the East Texas Kings' legacy continued to grow. They consistently performed well in regional and even national tournaments, earning the respect of their opponents and becoming a symbol of hope for other underdog teams.

But beyond the accolades and victories, the true essence of the Kings' story lay in the transformation of their players. Many of them, coming from diverse backgrounds and facing their own personal challenges, found a sense of purpose and direction through the program. The Kings became more than just a basketball team – they became a family, supporting each other through thick and thin, both on and off the court.

The rise of the underdogs was a testament to the power of dreams and the impact of a supportive community. It showed that with passion, hard work, and belief in oneself, anyone could rise from the shadows of obscurity to achieve greatness.

As the East Texas Kings Basketball Program, LLC continued to inspire young athletes, Coach Michael Thompson knew that their journey was far from over. The underdogs had risen, but their story had just begun. The world awaited the next chapter in the Kings' legacy – a story of continued growth, determination, and the pursuit of excellence. And so, they marched forward, carrying the spirit of underdogs turned champions in their hearts, ready to face whatever challenges lay ahead.

Chapter Four: Overcoming Adversity

The journey of the East Texas Kings Basketball Program, LLC was not without its share of challenges. As the team continued to rise and gain recognition, they faced adversity that tested their resilience and determination. But true to their spirit, the Kings embraced each obstacle as an opportunity to grow and learn, proving that champions were not defined by their victories alone, but by how they faced adversity.

One of the most significant challenges came during a critical season when the Kings' star player, Jarell Greene, suffered a serious injury during a crucial game. Jarell was not only a key player on the team but also a source of inspiration for his teammates. The news of his injury sent shockwaves through the entire program.

Coach Justiss gathered the team to address the situation. He reminded them that adversity was an inevitable part of any journey to success, and it was their response to it that would define their character. He urged the players to rally around Jarell and support him during his recovery, knowing that his absence on the court would be felt deeply.

The Kings faced a string of losses in the immediate aftermath of Jarell's injury. Without their star player, they struggled to find their footing on the court. Doubts crept into the minds of some players, and morale began to waver.

But Coach Justiss refused to let adversity define them. He encouraged the team to view Jarell's injury as an opportunity for others to step up and take on leadership roles. Each player was reminded of the unique strengths they brought to the team and how they could make a difference in their own way.

As the team adapted to playing without Jarell, a newfound sense of unity emerged. They realized that they were stronger together, and the belief in themselves and each other began to grow once more.

To further strengthen their bond, the Kings engaged in team-building activities outside of basketball. They participated in community service projects, volunteering their time to support local charities and schools. This not only brought them closer as a team, but also reminded them of the impact they could have on their community beyond the basketball court.

As Jarell progressed in his recovery, he became a source of inspiration for the team. His resilience and determination to return to the court motivated everyone to give their best, knowing that their star player was fighting to be back with them.

In a crucial game later in the season, the Kings faced off against a fierce rival team. It was a back-and-forth battle, with both teams refusing to back down. In the final minutes of the game, the score was tied, and the pressure was on.

With Jarell back on the sidelines, the Kings drew strength from his presence. They played with an unwavering focus, executing their plays flawlessly. As the clock wound down, a young and talented player named Kayden, who had stepped up in Jarell's absence, made a clutch shot that secured a thrilling victory for the Kings.

The joy and sense of accomplishment that followed that game were unmatched. The Kings had not only overcome adversity but had triumphed against all odds. They had proven that their success was not solely reliant on any single player but on the collective effort of the team as a whole.

The journey of overcoming adversity did not end with that victory. The Kings understood that challenges would always be a part of their journey, but they had learned how to face them with courage and determination. Each obstacle they encountered served as a reminder of their growth and the unbreakable bond that united them as a team.

As the East Texas Kings Basketball Program LLC continued to evolve, they knew that the path to success was not linear. It was marked by ups and downs, victories and defeats, but most importantly, by a spirit that refused to be broken. The Kings had become more than just champions on the court; they had become champions in life, showing the world that with perseverance and a united heart, they could overcome any adversity that came their way.

Chapter Five: The Championship Run

As the East Texas Kings Basketball Program, LLC continued to grow and overcome adversity, they set their sights on the ultimate goal – a championship title. The dream that had started as a flicker in the heart of Coach Justiss Hill was now a burning desire in the hearts of every player on the team.

With each passing season, the Kings' skill, unity, and reputation soared to new heights. They became a formidable force in the region, earning the respect of their competitors and drawing in larger crowds to their games. Their dedication to skill development, academic excellence, and character building set them apart from other teams, making them a force to be reckoned with both on and off the court.

The Kings qualified for the state championships, where they faced the best teams from all over Texas. It was an exhilarating yet nerve-wracking experience. Their journey had brought them to the grandest stage in high school basketball, and they were determined to leave a lasting mark.

In the first few games of the tournament, the Kings showed their dominance, securing convincing victories and advancing to the later rounds. Their chemistry and unselfish play were evident, with every player embracing their role and contributing to the team's success.

As they progressed further in the tournament, the stakes grew higher, and the pressure mounted. Each game seemed like a battle, testing the Kings' mental fortitude and resolve. They faced teams with different styles of play, some of which they had never encountered before.

But the Kings were not about to back down. They drew strength from their journey, from the challenges they had faced and overcome together. Coach Hill reminded them of the countless hours of hard work and sacrifice they had put into their dream and encouraged them to leave everything on the court.

In the semi-finals, the Kings faced their most formidable opponents yet – a team with a record of dominance in the state championships. The game was intense, with both teams trading leads throughout. In the final minutes, the Kings found themselves trailing by a narrow margin.

It was a defining moment – a moment that called for something extraordinary. The Kings huddled together, their determination palpable. They knew that they had come too far to let this moment slip away.

In the final seconds of the game, a player named Mali, who had emerged as a star shooter during the tournament, made a clutch three-pointer that turned the tide in the Kings' favor. The crowd erupted in cheers as the Kings secured a dramatic victory, propelling them into the championship game.

The championship game was an epic battle that showcased the Kings' grit and determination. They faced a team with equal skill and passion, and it was a back-and-forth contest until the very end. But the Kings' resilience and unity proved to be the deciding factor.

In the final minutes, with the score tied, the Kings executed a perfectly coordinated play that led to a game-winning basket. The buzzer sounded, and the East Texas Kings Basketball Program, LLC had achieved the unimaginable – they were the state champions!

The celebrations that followed were filled with tears of joy and shouts of triumph. The players embraced one another, knowing that they had achieved something truly special. Their journey from underdogs to champions had come full circle, and they stood tall as living proof that dreams could become a reality.

As they hoisted the championship trophy, the Kings knew that this victory was about more than just basketball. It was a testament to the power of dreams, hard work, and the unwavering support of a community. They had become more than just a basketball team – they were a symbol of hope and inspiration to aspiring athletes everywhere.

The championship run of the East Texas Kings Basketball Program LLC was a story of triumph over adversity, of unity and determination prevailing against all odds. It was a story that would be told and celebrated for generations to come, inspiring countless young athletes to believe in their dreams and reach for the stars, just like the Kings had done. And so, with their heads held high and hearts full of pride, the East Texas Kings Basketball Program, LLC continued to write their story, embarking on new journeys, forever etching their legacy in the annals of basketball history.

Chapter Six: Impact Beyond the Court

The victory of the East Texas Kings Basketball Program, LLC in the state championships marked the pinnacle of their success on the court, but their impact reached far beyond the boundaries of the basketball court. The Kings had become a beacon of hope and inspiration, transforming lives and leaving an indelible mark on their community and beyond.

As news of their championship victory spread, the Kings received an outpouring of support and admiration from people all over the country. Their story resonated with many, inspiring young athletes and coaches alike to believe in the power of dreams and hard work.

One of the most significant impacts of the Kings' success was on the young athletes who were part of the program. The players had not only grown as basketball players but also as individuals. They had imbibed the values of discipline, perseverance, and teamwork, which transcended the basketball court and became guiding principles in their lives.

Many of the Kings' players went on to excel in college, not just in basketball but also in academics and other areas.

They became role models in their communities, showing others that with determination and support, anything was possible.

The success of the program also attracted more talented young athletes from the region and beyond. The East Texas Kings Basketball Program, LLC had become a destination for aspiring basketball players who sought to be part of a program that not only nurtured their skills but also fostered personal growth and character development.

Beyond the players, the impact of the Kings extended to the coaches, mentors, and volunteers who dedicated their time and expertise to the program. Witnessing the transformation of the young athletes filled their hearts with pride and reaffirmed their belief in the power of sports as a vehicle for positive change.

The Kings had also become advocates for community involvement and giving back. They engaged in various charity events, supporting causes that ranged from education and youth development to environmental conservation. Their actions inspired others to do the same, sparking a wave of community service and volunteerism in Pineville and neighboring towns.

The success of the Kings also caught the attention of businesses and organizations who recognized the value of supporting youth sports and community initiatives. Sponsorships and donations poured in, enabling the program to expand and offer more scholarships to deserving athletes, regardless of their financial background.

Coach Justiss Hill's dream had grown beyond anything he had initially envisioned. The East Texas Kings Basketball Program, LLC had become a force for positive change in the community, shaping the lives of young athletes and inspiring others to dream big and work hard.

The Kings' story was featured in newspapers, magazines, and television programs, spreading their message of hope and determination to a wider audience. Coach Justiss and the team were invited to speak at various conferences and events, sharing their journey and inspiring others with their story.

Their impact was not confined to their local community. Other youth basketball programs and coaches looked up to the Kings as a model of success, seeking advice and guidance on how to build a program that made a difference beyond wins and losses.

As the years passed, the East Texas Kings Basketball Program, LLC continued to make an impact. They knew that their journey was ongoing, and their story was far from over. The Kings understood that the true measure of success lay in their ability to continue inspiring and empowering young athletes for generations to come.

And so, with hearts full of gratitude and determination, the East Texas Kings Basketball Program, LLC marched forward, forever carrying the spirit of underdogs turned champions and champions turned agents of positive change. Their legacy was etched not just on the basketball court but in the hearts and minds of all those whose lives they had touched.

Chapter Seven: Legacy and Future

The legacy of the East Texas Kings Basketball Program, LLC was etched into the hearts and minds of the community, leaving an enduring impact that extended far beyond the confines of a basketball court. Their story of underdogs turned champions and champions turned agents of positive change had become a source of inspiration for generations to come.

The program's success continued to thrive long after their championship victory. The Kings consistently produced talented basketball players who went on to excel not only in college but also in professional leagues. Their alumni were not just skilled athletes but also leaders in various fields, making a mark in business, education, and community development.

Coach Justiss Hill had become a revered figure in the basketball community. His dedication to nurturing young athletes and instilling values beyond the game earned him numerous accolades and awards. He remained committed to the program, guiding it with the same passion and vision that had driven him from the beginning.

The impact of the East Texas Kings Basketball Program, LLC had transcended geographical boundaries. Other communities and sports programs looked up to them as a model of success, seeking guidance on building programs that focused on holistic development and community engagement.

The Kings' training facility had expanded, becoming a state-of-the-art center of excellence for basketball. It not only catered to the needs of their own athletes but also served as a hub for basketball enthusiasts from all around Texas. The facility hosted basketball camps, clinics, and tournaments, welcoming players of all ages and skill levels.

Through scholarships and outreach programs, the Kings had created opportunities for underprivileged youth to be part of the program. The vision of inclusivity and providing equal access to opportunities had become an integral part of their legacy.

Beyond basketball, the Kings continued to make a difference in their community through various philanthropic endeavors. They collaborated with local organizations, supporting initiatives that focused on education, health, and environmental sustainability. The program had become a driving force for positive change in the region, inspiring a ripple effect of community service and civic engagement.

As the East Texas Kings Basketball Program, LLC looked to the future, they remained committed to their core values and the belief that their journey was an ongoing one. They understood that the pursuit of excellence was a continuous endeavor, and their legacy was built on the foundation of hard work, unity, and a commitment to making a difference in the lives of others.

The program sought to expand its reach, establishing partnerships with other sports programs and organizations to create more opportunities for youth across various disciplines. They believed in the power of sports to foster personal growth and development, regardless of the chosen field.

With each passing year, new faces joined the Kings, each one adding to the rich tapestry of their legacy. The program's alumni, scattered across the world, remained connected to their roots, serving as mentors and role models to the next generation of Kings.

The East Texas Kings Basketball Program, LLC had become more than just a team or an organization; it had become a movement – a movement of empowerment, transformation, and positive change. Their legacy was woven into the fabric of their community, a story of dreams achieved, and lives transformed.

As they looked toward the future, the Kings remained guided by the same principles that had brought them this far – the belief in the potential of every young athlete, the power of teamwork and unity, and the importance of giving back to the community that had supported them throughout their journey.

And so, with hearts full of gratitude, determination, and a spirit that refused to be contained, the East Texas Kings Basketball Program LLC continued to march forward, forever leaving their mark on the world, one inspired and empowered athlete at a time. Their legacy, like the echoes of a champion's victory, reverberated through time, inspiring countless dreams and forging a path of excellence for generations to come.

Chapter Eight: The Power of Unity

The East Texas Kings Basketball Program, LLC had achieved great success, but their triumphs were not solely attributed to individual talent or skills. The true secret of their success lay in the power of unity – the unbreakable bond that bound them together as a team and as a family.

Throughout their journey, the Kings had learned that success was not just about a one star player or a single moment of brilliance. It was about the collective effort of every player, coach, and supporter who contributed their unique strengths and talents to the team's success.

The power of unity was evident in the way the players supported each other on and off the court. They celebrated each other's successes and lifted each other up during challenging times. The Kings knew that they were stronger together, and that belief fueled their determination to conquer any obstacle that came their way.

Coach Justiss Hill had fostered a culture of trust and respect within the team. He encouraged open communication, ensuring that every player's voice was heard and valued. This inclusivity bred a sense of ownership and commitment among the players, making them feel invested in the program's success.

Unity extended beyond the boundaries of the basketball court and into the community. The Kings became ambassadors of togetherness, inspiring people from different walks of life to come together in support of a common goal. They embraced the diversity within their team and celebrated the unique backgrounds and experiences that each player brought to the table.

The power of unity was showcased during the championship run. It was not just about the final victory but the journey they had undertaken together. The Kings had faced setbacks, injuries, and tough competition, but they never wavered in their belief in each other.

In a crucial moment during the championship game, when the pressure was at its peak, the Kings exemplified the power of unity. They executed a perfectly coordinated play that resulted in the game-winning shot. It was a testament to their trust in one another and their ability to work as a cohesive unit.

Their triumph in the state championships was a reflection of the power of unity, not only on the basketball court, but in their community as well. The support they received from the Naples community and beyond was a testament to the impact they had made through their collective efforts.

The power of unity also extended to the alumni of the program. Former players continued to support and mentor the current team, forming a close-knit network that strengthened the Kings' legacy. They understood the importance of giving back and supporting the next generation of aspiring athletes.

The Kings' success had become a source of pride for the entire East Texas community. Their unity and perseverance had brought people together, uniting them behind a common cause and inspiring them to believe in the power of dreams.

As they looked to the future, the East Texas Kings Basketball Program, LLC knew that the power of unity would remain at the core of their journey. They understood that no matter the challenges that lay ahead, they could overcome them through collective effort, trust, and support.

Their legacy was not just about championships or accolades but about the impact they had on the lives of the young athletes they nurtured. The lessons of unity, determination, and community engagement had become ingrained in the hearts of every player who had been part of the Kings' family.

And so, with hearts united in purpose and minds focused on a brighter future, the East Texas Kings Basketball Program LLC continued to march forward, knowing that the power of unity was their most potent weapon, capable of conquering any obstacle and inspiring the world to dream big, work together, and create positive change.

Chapter Nine: The Heart of a Champion

The heart of a champion beats within each member of the East Texas Kings Basketball Program, LLC. It is a heart that knows no boundaries, fueled by a passion for the game, a commitment to excellence, and a spirit that refuses to be defeated.

For the Kings, being a champion was not just about winning games or trophies. It was about embodying the values of hard work, integrity, and the power of unity that had carried them through their journey. The heart of a champion was about facing adversity with courage, using setbacks as stepping stones, and believing in oneself and each other.

The heart of a champion was reflected in the dedication of Coach Justiss Hill, whose unwavering belief in the potential of every player had transformed the lives of countless young athletes. His heart beat in sync with the pulse of the team, inspiring them to reach heights they had never imagined possible.

As the Kings continued their journey, they encountered new challenges and obstacles. But the heart of a champion knew no fear. It beat stronger with every setback, motivating the players to dig deeper, work harder, and never give up.

In the face of tough competition, the Kings displayed the heart of a champion by approaching each game with humility and respect for their opponents. They understood that true greatness was not just about individual talent but about the ability to uplift and inspire others.

The heart of a champion was evident in the selflessness of the players, who celebrated each other's successes as if they were their own. They understood that the strength of the team lay in their collective spirit and their willingness to lift each other up.

Their journey of success was not without its challenges, but the heart of a champion knew how to turn setbacks into opportunities for growth. Each defeat became a lesson, and each victory was celebrated with humility. The Kings understood that true champions were defined not just by their triumphs but by their response to adversity.

The heart of a champion extended beyond the basketball court and into their community. The Kings used their platform to inspire positive change, engaging in community service and supporting causes that mattered to them. They knew that being a champion was not just about personal success but about making a difference in the lives of others.

As the Kings looked to the future, the heart of a champion continued to beat within them, guiding their every step. They knew that their journey was ongoing, and their legacy was not defined by a single moment but by the impact they had on the lives of young athletes and the community they served.

Their success had become a beacon of hope and inspiration for aspiring athletes everywhere. The heart of a champion reminded them that greatness was not reserved for a select few but was attainable by anyone willing to embrace the values of dedication, perseverance, and teamwork.

And so, with the heart of a champion as their compass, the East Texas Kings Basketball Program, LLC continued to march forward, forever carrying the spirit of underdogs turned champions and champions turned agents of positive change. Their legacy was etched not just on the basketball court but in the hearts and minds of all those whose lives they had touched. For the heart of a champion beats not just in victory but in the journey itself, forever driving them to reach for the stars and inspire others to do the same.

Chapter Ten: Celebrating Success

The East Texas Kings Basketball Program, LLC had come a long way from its humble beginnings. Their journey from underdogs to champions had been marked by hard work, determination, and the unwavering support of their community. Now, it was time for the Kings to celebrate their success and reflect on the impact they had made.

The championship victory had ignited a wave of joy and pride in Pineville and beyond. The entire community rallied behind the Kings, celebrating their triumph as if it were their own. The streets were adorned with banners and posters, and a grand parade was organized to honor the team and their achievements.

The celebration was not just about the championship trophy; it was about acknowledging the heart, soul, and effort the Kings had poured into their journey. It was a testament to the power of dreams, hard work, and unity – qualities that had become ingrained in the fabric of the program.

During the celebration, Coach Michael Thompson addressed the crowd, expressing his gratitude to the community for their unwavering support. He emphasized that the Kings' success was not just about basketball but about the values they had upheld throughout their journey.

The players, each with a glimmer of pride in their eyes, also took the stage to share their experiences. They thanked their families, coaches, and teammates for believing in them and supporting them through thick and thin. Their speeches were filled with humility and gratitude, a reflection of the heart of a champion that beat within each of them.

As the celebration continued, the Kings' alumni returned to Pineville from various parts of the country to be part of the festivities. The reunion was a heartwarming sight as former players, now successful in their own right, came together to celebrate the legacy they had helped build.

The impact of the Kings' success went beyond their community. They received messages of congratulations and admiration from basketball enthusiasts and sports organizations from around the country. Their story was featured in newspapers, magazines, and sports documentaries, spreading their message of inspiration and empowerment to a wider audience.

But amidst the celebration, the Kings remained grounded, knowing that their journey was ongoing. They understood that true success was not just about one moment but about the continued pursuit of excellence, both on and off the court.

As they looked to the future, the Kings remained committed to their values and their mission of making a positive impact on young athletes and their community. They knew that their legacy was not just about championships and trophies but about the lives they had touched and the dreams they had ignited.

The celebration was a testament to the power of dreams, hard work, and unity. It was a celebration of the heart of a champion that beat within every member of the East Texas Kings Basketball Program, LLC. Their journey had left an indelible mark on the world, inspiring countless dreams and forging a path of excellence for generations to come.

And so, with hearts full of gratitude, determination, and the spirit of celebration, the East Texas Kings Basketball Program, LLC continued to march forward, forever leaving their mark on the world, one inspired and empowered athlete at a time. For the heart of a champion knows no bounds and celebrates not just success but the journey itself, forever inspiring others to dream big, work together, and create positive change.

Chapter Eleven: Lessons Learned

The journey of the East Texas Kings Basketball Program, LLC had been a remarkable one, filled with triumphs, challenges, and moments of inspiration. Along the way, they had learned valuable lessons that shaped their character, their approach to the game, and their impact on the community. Here are some of the key lessons the Kings had learned:

The Power of Dreams: The journey had started with a dream in Coach Michael Thompson's heart. The Kings learned that dreams were powerful motivators that could push them beyond their limits. They realized that by believing in their dreams and working tirelessly to achieve them, they could turn the impossible into reality.

Hard Work and Perseverance: Success was not handed to the Kings on a silver platter. They learned that hard work, dedication, and a willingness to persevere through setbacks were essential for achieving greatness. Every player understood that success was not an overnight accomplishment but the result of continuous effort and improvement.

The Strength of Unity: The Kings realized that they were stronger together. Unity was not just about playing as a team on the court but supporting and uplifting each other off the court as well. The bond they forged as a team extended beyond basketball and became the heart of their success.

Embracing Adversity: The Kings learned that setbacks and challenges were part of any journey to success. They discovered the importance of embracing adversity, as it presented opportunities for growth and learning. Their ability to bounce back from setbacks and turn them into stepping stones was a testament to their resilience.

Impact Beyond the Game: The Kings understood that their impact went beyond the basketball court. They learned that sports could be a powerful tool for positive change in their community. They embraced the responsibility of being role models and used their platform to give back and make a difference.

Humility and Sportsmanship: Throughout their journey, the Kings remained humble in victory and gracious in defeat. They valued sportsmanship and respect for their opponents, understanding that true champions exemplified character both on and off the court.

The Importance of Community Support: The unwavering support of their community had been crucial to the Kings' success. They learned that success was not an individual achievement but a collective effort that involved the entire community. The love and encouragement they received from their families, friends, and fans were the fuel that propelled them forward.

Leading by Example: Coach Michael Thompson's leadership played a pivotal role in the success of the program. The Kings learned the importance of leading by example, not just through words but through actions. Coach Michael's dedication and passion inspired them to give their best and be the best versions of themselves.

Continual Growth and Improvement: The Kings understood that the pursuit of excellence was a never-ending journey. They learned that there was always room for growth and improvement, both as athletes and as individuals. They embraced the challenge of constantly pushing their limits and striving for better results.

Leaving a Legacy: The Kings realized that their journey was not just about the present but about leaving a legacy for future generations. They learned the importance of being role models and inspiring others to dream big and believe in themselves.

As the East Texas Kings Basketball Program, LLC looked to the future, they carried these lessons in their hearts. Their journey had not just been about basketball; it had been about transformation, empowerment, and making a positive impact on the world. With their heads held high and hearts full of gratitude, determination, and the wisdom of the lessons learned, the Kings continued to march forward, forever leaving their mark on the world, one inspired and empowered athlete at a time.

Chapter Twelve: Underdogs to Champions

In the heart of East Texas, where dreams met reality on the basketball court, the journey of the East Texas Kings Basketball Program, LLC continued to unfold. The echoes of the past struggles still lingered, but the fire of determination burned brighter than ever before. It was a journey from underdogs to champions, a transformation that defined the essence of the team's spirit.

Facing Adversity: The path to becoming champions was not paved with ease. The Kings confronted adversities that tested their resolve and commitment. They encountered defeats that could have shattered their spirits, but they chose to see them as stepping stones toward growth.

Unity Amidst Challenges: In the face of challenges, the Kings embraced unity. The belief that they were stronger together than as individuals fueled their perseverance. The locker room wasn't just a place to change uniforms; it was a sanctuary of shared dreams and unwavering support.

Turning Points: Every journey to greatness is marked by turning points. For the Kings, it was a pivotal game that ignited a fire within them. It was the game they rallied from behind, showing the world that their underdog status was not a limitation but a source of determination.

Learning from Defeat: Defeat wasn't an end; it was a lesson. The Kings used losses as opportunities to learn, to reevaluate their strategies, and to emerge even stronger. Each setback became a catalyst for their rise.

Unwavering Belief: Amidst the doubts and naysayers, the Kings held onto an unwavering belief in themselves. They carried a vision of their future success, fueled by their dedication to their craft and their community.

The Spark of Inspiration: The Kings' journey from underdogs to champions became an inspiration for the entire community. The sight of local athletes triumphing against the odds ignited dreams in the hearts of young players, parents, and supporters alike.

Humility in Victory: As the Kings tasted victory, they remained grounded in humility. The lessons of their underdog days never left them, reminding them that success was a privilege to be earned anew with every game.

Continuing the Journey: The journey from underdogs to champions was not a destination but a process. The Kings understood that the path to success was marked by continuous growth, both on and off the court.

<u>Heart of a Champion:</u> The heart of a champion wasn't just about winning; it was about the unwavering determination to rise, the resilience to face challenges, and the commitment to inspire others through their journey.

As Chapter Twelve closed it's pages, the story of the East Texas Kings Basketball Program LLC continued to unfold. Their journey, with its triumphs and trials, was a testament to the power of dreams, unity, and unwavering determination. The next chapters held even more challenges, victories, and life lessons as the Kings embraced their role as champions, not just in basketball but in life itself.

From Underdogs To Champions

Chapter Thirteen: Embracing Change

As the East Texas Kings Basketball Program, LLC looked ahead to the future, they understood that change was an inevitable part of their journey. Embracing change was crucial for their continued growth and success. They knew that by adapting to new circumstances and challenges, they could remain at the forefront of positive transformation in their community and beyond.

One of the first changes the Kings embraced was the expansion of their program. With their increasing impact and reputation, the demand for participation grew. They welcomed new players, coaches, and volunteers into the Kings' family, creating a more diverse and inclusive community.

As they expanded, the Kings maintained their commitment to developing young athletes not just as basketball players but as well-rounded individuals. They focused on character building, leadership skills, and academic excellence, understanding that these qualities were essential for success both on and off the court.

The program also embraced changes in training methods and technology. They continuously sought new ways to improve player development, using data analytics and sports science to enhance performance. The Kings understood that staying ahead in the competitive world of sports required a willingness to adapt to new advancements.

As they faced changes in the sports landscape, the Kings remained true to their core values. They understood that while change was essential, their foundation of unity, hard work, and community engagement remained constant. They continued to prioritize the power of teamwork and the positive impact they could have on their community.

Embracing change also meant exploring opportunities for collaboration and partnerships. The Kings sought alliances with like-minded organizations that shared their values and vision for positive change. Through these collaborations, they were able to extend their reach and make a broader impact.

The Kings also embraced changes in their philanthropic efforts. They actively sought out causes and projects that aligned with their mission of empowerment and community development. Whether it was supporting education initiatives, environmental conservation, or youth outreach programs, the Kings were committed to making a difference beyond the basketball court.

As the program expanded, they faced the challenge of maintaining a sense of family and unity. The Kings recognized the importance of fostering strong relationships among players, coaches, and volunteers. They organized team-building activities, retreats, and community events that reinforced their bond and kept the family spirit alive.

Beyond the Kings' journey, change also came in the form of new talent and emerging stars in the basketball world. The Kings welcomed fresh talent and celebrated the achievements of others, recognizing that competition pushed them to be even better versions of themselves.

As the East Texas Kings Basketball Program, LLC embraced change, they remained mindful of their roots and the lessons learned along their journey. The heart of a champion beat within them, propelling them forward with the knowledge that change was an opportunity for growth, not a reason to fear.

In times of change, the Kings found strength in their unity. Together, they faced challenges head-on and overcame them with determination and resilience. The heart of a champion knew that change was not an obstacle but a chance to evolve and thrive.

And so, with open hearts and minds, the East Texas Kings Basketball Program, LLC continued to march forward. They embraced change as a catalyst for progress and innovation, forever leaving their mark on the world and inspiring countless dreams with the enduring spirit of unity, empowerment, and the heart of a champion.

Chapter Fourteen: Sustaining Success

Sustaining success was a top priority for the East Texas Kings Basketball Program, LLC. They understood that achieving greatness was just the beginning, and true success lay in maintaining their impact and legacy over time. To sustain their success, the Kings focused on several key elements:

Continuous Improvement: The Kings never rested on their laurels. They embraced a culture of continuous improvement, both as individuals and as a team. They encouraged feedback, analyzed their performance, and sought ways to enhance their skills and strategies.

Evolving Leadership: Coach Michael Thompson knew that as the program grew, leadership would play a critical role in sustaining success. He groomed and empowered assistant coaches to take on more responsibilities, ensuring a smooth transition in the future.

Investing in Youth Development: The Kings recognized that the future of their program relied on nurturing young talent. They established youth development programs and grassroots initiatives to identify and groom potential players from a young age.

Alumni Engagement: The Kings maintained strong ties with their alumni, involving them in mentoring, coaching, and community outreach efforts. The support and guidance of former players played a crucial role in sustaining the program's values and legacy.

Adapting to Changing Times: The Kings remained open to change, embracing new technology, training methods, and strategies. They adapted to the evolving landscape of sports to stay competitive and relevant in the ever-changing world of basketball.

Community Involvement: The Kings understood that their success was intertwined with the support of their community. They continued to give back, engaging in community service and collaborating with local organizations to address pressing needs.

Cultivating Team Chemistry: The Kings recognized that their unity as a team was a significant factor in their success. They continued to prioritize team-building activities and a supportive team culture to maintain their strong bond.

Balancing Tradition and Innovation: While the Kings embraced innovation, they also valued their traditions and the core values that had brought them success. They struck a balance between embracing new ideas and preserving their identity.

Fostering a Growth Mindset: The Kings instilled a growth mindset in every player and coach, encouraging them to see challenges as opportunities for learning and growth. They celebrated effort, resilience, and perseverance as much as they celebrated victories.

Long-Term Planning: The Kings developed a strategic vision for the future, setting long-term goals and outlining a roadmap for sustained success. They understood that staying focused on their mission and vision was essential in the face of challenges.

By focusing on these elements, the East Texas Kings Basketball Program, LLC continued to thrive and make a lasting impact. Their journey was not about short-term triumphs but about leaving a legacy that would endure for generations to come.

As they looked to the future, the Kings knew that sustaining success required unwavering commitment, dedication, and the heart of a champion. They remained driven by the belief that their impact extended beyond basketball, inspiring others to dream big and make a positive difference in their communities.

And so, with hearts filled with gratitude, determination, and the wisdom gained from their journey, the East Texas Kings Basketball Program LLC continued to march forward, forever leaving their mark on the world, one inspired and empowered athlete at a time. For the heart of a champion knows no limits and sustains success not just for the present but for the future, forever shining as a beacon of hope, unity, and the power of dreams.

Chapter Fifteen: The Power of Mentorship

The East Texas Kings Basketball Program, LLC understood the immense power of mentorship in shaping the lives of young athletes. Throughout their journey, mentorship had been a cornerstone of their success, instilling in the players the values, skills, and guidance needed to thrive on and off the court.

Coach Michael Thompson knew the significance of mentorship from the very beginning. As a mentor himself, he believed in the transformative impact that a strong mentor could have on a young athlete's life. He sought to create an environment where every player had access to positive role models and mentors who would inspire and guide them.

The mentorship within the Kings extended beyond Coach Michael. Assistant coaches, team captains, and alumni all played vital roles as mentors to the younger players. They shared their experiences, provided advice, and served as a support system for the entire team.

Mentorship wasn't just about imparting basketball skills; it was about nurturing personal growth and character development. Mentors encouraged players to set goals, work hard, and embrace challenges. They taught the importance of resilience, discipline, and the value of teamwork.

One-on-one mentorship sessions became a regular part of the program's activities. Players were given the opportunity to discuss their aspirations, concerns, and personal challenges with their mentors. These conversations helped build trust and fostered a sense of belonging within the Kings' family.

Mentorship also extended into the community. The Kings recognized the importance of giving back and serving as mentors to young athletes beyond their program. They engaged in outreach initiatives, visiting schools, and community centers to inspire and encourage the next generation of athletes.

As the Kings' alumni succeeded in their own careers, many returned to mentor the current players. Their success stories served as a powerful reminder that dreams were attainable with hard work and dedication. Alumni mentors shared their experiences of overcoming challenges, further inspiring the young athletes to pursue their goals.

Beyond basketball skills, mentors also focused on life skills such as time management, communication, and leadership. They emphasized the importance of education and encouraged players to excel academically. Mentorship had a holistic approach, nurturing every aspect of the players' development.

The impact of mentorship went beyond the duration of a player's time with the Kings. Many players continued to seek guidance from their mentors long after they had moved on from the program. The relationships forged through mentorship remained enduring and served as a lifelong source of inspiration and support.

The power of mentorship was not limited to the players alone. Coaches and mentors also found fulfillment and growth in the process. Guiding young athletes and witnessing their progress became a source of immense pride and motivation for everyone involved.

As the East Texas Kings Basketball Program, LLC looked to the future, they understood that mentorship would remain a fundamental element of their journey. The heart of a champion was built not just on individual talent but on the guidance and support provided by mentors who believed in the potential of every player.

And so, with hearts full of gratitude, determination, and the power of mentorship, the East Texas Kings Basketball Program, LLC continued to march forward, forever leaving their mark on the world, one inspired and empowered athlete at a time. For the heart of a champion beats with the guidance of mentors, forever driving them to reach for the stars and inspire others to do the same.

Chapter Sixteen: Facing New Rivals

As the East Texas Kings Basketball Program, LLC continued their journey, they knew that with success came new challenges and rivals. Their reputation as a dominant force in the basketball world had attracted the attention of other teams, eager to prove themselves against the reigning champions.

Facing new rivals meant that the Kings had to continually raise their level of play and stay ahead of the competition. Coach Justiss Hill understood that complacency was the enemy of sustained success. He motivated his players to stay hungry, to never settle for mediocrity, and to always strive for greatness.

The Kings embraced the challenge of facing new rivals with humility and respect. They recognized that every opponent was an opportunity to test their skills, learn from each game, and grow as a team. They approached every match with the same level of intensity, regardless of the opponent's reputation.

Coach Justiss Hill emphasized the importance of studying their rivals' strengths and weaknesses. He instilled a mindset of preparation and adaptability within the team. The Kings understood that knowing their opponents inside out was crucial for devising effective strategies on the court.

As the Kings faced new rivals, they were no longer the underdogs they once were. They had a target on their backs, and every team wanted to defeat the reigning champions. This motivated the Kings even more, as they understood that every victory they achieved was hard-earned and well-deserved.

The pressure of being champions did not deter the Kings. They embraced the expectations and used them as fuel to perform at their best. They knew that the heart of a champion was not just about winning titles but about consistently giving their all and never backing down from any challenge.

Facing new rivals also meant that the Kings had to continually evolve their style of play. They adapted their strategies based on the strengths and weaknesses of their opponents. Coach Hill encouraged creativity and innovation on the court, enabling the players to think on their feet and make split-second decisions.

Despite the competition, the Kings remained true to their core values. They continued to prioritize unity, sportsmanship, and community engagement. They knew that their legacy was about more than just winning games; it was about leaving a positive impact on and off the court.

The rivalry between the Kings and their competitors also served as a source of inspiration for young athletes. As the Kings faced tough opponents and overcame challenges, they demonstrated the heart of a champion to aspiring players, inspiring them to dream big and work hard. As the East Texas Kings Basketball Program, LLC faced new rivals, they did so with the same passion, determination, and unity that had brought them this far. They knew that their journey was not just about individual achievements but about the collective effort and the impact they had on their community.

And so, with hearts full of gratitude, determination, and the spirit of competition, the East Texas Kings Basketball Program LLC continued to march forward, forever leaving their mark on the world, one inspired and empowered athlete at a time. For the heart of a champion knows no fear in facing new rivals, forever embracing challenges as stepping stones toward continued success and growth.

Chapter Seventeen:
Balancing Basketball and Academics

For the student-athletes of the East Texas Kings Basketball Program, LLC, balancing the demands of basketball and academics was a priority. They understood that success on the court should not come at the expense of their education. Coach Justiss Hill emphasized the importance of excelling both as athletes and as students, knowing that a well-rounded education was crucial for their future.

Time Management: Balancing basketball and academics required effective time management. The players learned to create schedules that allowed them to dedicate sufficient time to both their studies and their training. They prioritized their commitments, ensuring that they could excel in both areas.

Academic Support: The Kings provided academic support to their players, recognizing that some may need extra assistance with their studies. Tutors and study groups were available to help players stay on top of their schoolwork and perform well academically.

Encouraging Excellence: Coach Thompson encouraged excellence both on and off the court. He celebrated academic achievements and recognized outstanding performance in the classroom. The Kings understood that being a champion was not just about basketball but about excelling in all aspects of life.

Creating a Supportive Environment: The Kings fostered a supportive environment where players felt comfortable discussing any challenges they faced with balancing their academic and athletic responsibilities. This open communication helped players receive the necessary support and guidance.

Stress Management: Balancing basketball and academics could be stressful at times. The Kings emphasized the importance of stress management techniques such as mindfulness, meditation, and maintaining a healthy work-life balance.

Setting Realistic Goals: The players set realistic academic and athletic goals for themselves. They understood that they couldn't excel in both areas overnight and that it required consistent effort and dedication. Setting achievable goals helped them stay motivated and focused.

Instilling a Growth Mindset: The Kings embraced a growth mindset, understanding that they could continually improve both as athletes and as students. They viewed challenges as opportunities for learning and used setbacks as motivation to work harder.

Support from Teachers and School Administrators: The Kings worked closely with teachers and school administrators to ensure that their academic needs were met. Teachers were understanding of their basketball commitments and provided the necessary flexibility when needed.

Celebrating Academic Achievements: The program celebrated academic achievements with the same enthusiasm as athletic victories. Recognizing academic excellence reinforced the message that education was a crucial aspect of the players' development.

Long-Term Planning: The Kings encouraged players to think about their future beyond basketball. They emphasized the importance of having academic and career goals and how education would play a pivotal role in their future success.

By prioritizing both basketball and academics, the East Texas Kings Basketball Program, LLC ensured that their players were well-prepared for life beyond the court. They knew that a strong academic foundation complemented their athletic abilities and empowered the players to achieve greatness in all aspects of life.

And so, with hearts full of dedication, gratitude, and the wisdom of balancing basketball and academics, the East Texas Kings Basketball Program, LLC continued to march forward, forever leaving their mark on the world, one inspired and empowered student-athlete at a time. For the heart of a champion knows that true success lies not just in winning games but in becoming well-rounded individuals who excel both on and off the court.

Chapter Eighteen:
The Power of Community Support

The East Texas Kings Basketball Program LLC understood that their success and impact were deeply rooted in the unwavering support of their community. Throughout their journey, the power of community support had been instrumental in propelling the Kings to new heights and making a positive difference in the lives of young athletes.

Rallying Behind a Dream: From the program's inception, the Naples, Texas community rallied behind Coach Justiss Hill's dream of creating a basketball program that would empower young athletes. The support was not just financial; it was a genuine belief in the vision and the potential impact on the community.

Fundraising and Sponsorship: The Kings received financial support through fundraising events, sponsorships from local businesses, and individual donations. The community understood the value of investing in the future of their young athletes and contributed wholeheartedly.

Packing the Stands: During games, the stands were always packed with enthusiastic fans, cheering on the Kings with unwavering support. The players fed off the energy of the crowd, and the community's passion for basketball was evident in their dedication to the team.

Community Engagement: The Kings actively engaged with the community through outreach programs, basketball clinics, and charity events. They visited schools, community centers, and hospitals to inspire and uplift the young members of their community.

Shared Sense of Pride: The success of the Kings became a source of immense pride for the entire community. Their achievements were celebrated as a collective triumph, and the players became role models for aspiring athletes.

Mentors and Role Models: The Kings were not just supported by the community; they also served as mentors and role models for young athletes in Pineville. The players understood the responsibility that came with their platform and inspired the next generation to dream big.

Overcoming Adversity Together: The community stood by the Kings during tough times, supporting them through losses and setbacks. The sense of solidarity helped the players bounce back stronger and more determined.

Building Bridges: The Kings used their platform to build bridges between different segments of the community. They promoted diversity and inclusion, bringing people together through the love of basketball.

Inspiring Volunteerism: The success of the Kings inspired community members to volunteer and get involved in local initiatives. The program's positive impact extended beyond the basketball court, touching various aspects of community life.

Leaving a Lasting Legacy: The power of community support ensured that the legacy of the Kings would endure for generations to come. The values they upheld and the positive impact they made on their community would continue to shape the lives of young athletes long after their time on the court.

As the East Texas Kings Basketball Program, LLC continued their journey, they were grateful for the unwavering support of their community. They understood that their success was a shared triumph, made possible by the collective efforts and belief of those around them.

And so, with hearts full of gratitude, determination, and the power of community support, the East Texas Kings Basketball Program, LLC continued to march forward, forever leaving their mark on the world, one inspired and empowered athlete at a time. For the heart of a champion beats in harmony with the support of their community, forever forging a bond that transcends basketball and creates positive change in the world.

Chapter Nineteen: Overcoming Self-Doubt

As the East Texas Kings Basketball Program, LLC continued their journey, they understood that self-doubt could be a formidable opponent. Even the most talented athletes sometimes grappled with uncertainty and insecurities. Coach Michael Thompson recognized the importance of helping his players overcome self-doubt and harness their full potential.

Cultivating a Positive Mindset: The Kings emphasized the power of positive thinking. They encouraged players to replace negative thoughts with affirmations and to visualize success on the court. A positive mindset allowed them to approach challenges with confidence and determination.

Embracing Failure as a Stepping Stone: Coach Hill reminded his players that failure was a natural part of the journey to success. Instead of being discouraged by setbacks, the Kings saw them as opportunities to learn and grow. They understood that each defeat brought valuable lessons for improvement.

Supportive Team Environment: The Kings fostered a supportive team environment where players encouraged and uplifted one another. The sense of unity helped individuals overcome self-doubt, knowing that their teammates had their backs.

Setting Realistic Goals: Coach Philly encouraged players to set realistic and achievable goals. Breaking down larger objectives into smaller, manageable steps helped players build confidence as they saw progress in their performance.

Focus on the Process, Not Just the Outcome: The Kings emphasized the importance of focusing on the process of improvement rather than solely fixating on winning or losing. By dedicating themselves to continuous growth, they reduced the pressure of immediate results.

Learning from Role Models: Coach Hill shared stories of athletes who had overcome self-doubt and achieved greatness. Learning from the experiences of role models provided inspiration and reassurance that self-doubt was a hurdle that could be conquered.

Encouragement and Constructive Feedback: The Kings provided constructive feedback to players while emphasizing their strengths and areas of improvement.

Encouragement helped players build confidence in their abilities and encouraged them to work through challenges.

<u>Developing Mental Resilience:</u> The Kings integrated mental resilience training into their practices. Techniques such as mindfulness, visualization, and breathing exercises helped players stay focused and composed during high-pressure situations.

<u>Celebrating Personal Growth:</u> The Kings celebrated personal growth and progress as much as they celebrated victories. Recognizing the effort and dedication players put into overcoming self-doubt reinforced their belief in their abilities.

<u>Support from Coaches and Mentors:</u> Coach Thompson and the coaching staff were always available to provide support and guidance to players facing self-doubt. Knowing they had a strong support system motivated players to persevere through difficult times.

As the East Texas Kings Basketball Program, LLC continued to overcome self-doubt, they understood that it was a continuous journey. The heart of a champion knew that self-doubt might arise at various points, but it was not a permanent barrier to success.

By embracing a positive mindset, supporting each other, and focusing on growth and improvement, the Kings empowered themselves to face self-doubt head-on and conquer it. They knew that their journey was not just about basketball but about becoming resilient, confident individuals who could inspire and uplift others in their own struggles.

And so, with hearts full of determination, courage, and the wisdom of overcoming self-doubt, the East Texas Kings Basketball Program LLC continued to march forward, forever leaving their mark on the world, one inspired and empowered athlete at a time. For the heart of a champion knows that self-belief is the key to unlocking true greatness on and off the court.

Chapter Twenty: The Evolution of Leadership

Throughout their journey, the East Texas Kings Basketball Program, LLC experienced a significant evolution in leadership. As the program grew and faced new challenges, the role of leadership expanded beyond the court and the coaching staff. The evolution of leadership played a vital role in shaping the program's culture, values, and impact on the community.

Coach Michael Thompson's Vision: Coach Thompson's vision and passion were the driving force behind the program's inception. His leadership laid the foundation for the Kings' success, inspiring players and coaches alike to embody the heart of a champion.

Empowering Assistant Coaches: As the program expanded, Coach Thompson understood the importance of empowering his assistant coaches. He delegated more responsibilities to them, nurturing their growth as leaders and mentors to the players.

Alumni as Mentors: The Kings' alumni became integral to the program's leadership, serving as mentors and role models for the current players. Their experiences and insights provided invaluable guidance and inspiration.

Captains as Leaders: Team captains took on leadership roles both on and off the court. They exemplified the Kings' values, motivated their teammates, and facilitated communication between players and coaches.

Players as Leaders: The Kings fostered a culture where every player had the opportunity to be a leader, regardless of their position or playing time. Each player's unique strengths were valued, and their input was encouraged in team decisions.

Community Engagement: The evolution of leadership extended beyond the team, as the Kings became leaders in community engagement. They actively participated in local initiatives, using their platform to make a positive impact on their community.

Embracing Diversity: The evolving leadership within the Kings emphasized the importance of embracing diversity and inclusion. They celebrated the unique strengths and perspectives of each member, fostering a supportive and united team.

Leadership in Times of Adversity: The true test of leadership came during challenging times. The Kings' leaders displayed resilience, optimism, and determination, guiding the team through setbacks and motivating them to stay focused on their goals.

Balancing Individual and Team Leadership: The evolution of leadership struck a balance between individual and team leadership. While each player had the opportunity to lead, they understood that the team's success relied on cohesive, collective effort.

Leaving a Leadership Legacy: As senior players graduated and moved on, they left behind a leadership legacy for the next generation. The lessons learned and the culture they cultivated became the foundation for future leaders within the program.

As the East Texas Kings Basketball Program, LLC continued to evolve, they knew that leadership would remain a crucial aspect of their journey. They understood that the heart of a champion extended far beyond basketball skills; it encompassed the qualities of character, unity, and community engagement.

And so, with hearts full of gratitude, determination, and the evolution of leadership, the East Texas Kings Basketball Program LLC continued to march forward, forever leaving their mark on the world, one inspired and empowered leader at a time. For the heart of a champion knows that true leadership lies in empowering others and creating a lasting legacy of positive change in the world.

Chapter Twenty-One: The Power of Resilience

Resilience was a cornerstone of the East Texas Kings Basketball Program, LLC's journey. Throughout their pursuit of greatness, they faced numerous obstacles and setbacks, but their ability to bounce back and persevere made all the difference. The power of resilience propelled the Kings forward and transformed challenges into opportunities for growth and learning.

Embracing Challenges: The Kings understood that challenges were an inherent part of their journey. Instead of shying away from them, they embraced challenges with a positive mindset, viewing them as stepping stones toward improvement.

Learning from Setbacks: Every defeat and setback served as a valuable learning experience for the Kings. They analyzed their mistakes, identified areas for improvement, and used these lessons to refine their strategies.

Mental Toughness: The Kings developed mental toughness to navigate through high-pressure situations. They learned to stay composed, focused, and confident, even in the face of adversity.

<u>Supportive Environment:</u> The Kings fostered a supportive environment where players could lean on each other and their coaches during challenging times. The sense of unity provided strength and encouragement to overcome obstacles.

<u>Trusting the Process:</u> Coach Michael Thompson instilled a belief in trusting the process of improvement. He encouraged players to stay committed to their training and development, knowing that progress would come with dedication and perseverance.

<u>Resilient Leaders:</u> The Kings' leaders played a pivotal role in instilling resilience within the team. Captains and veteran players led by example, showing younger athletes how to handle adversity with grace and determination.

<u>Focus on Growth, Not Perfection:</u> Rather than seeking perfection, the Kings focused on continuous growth. They understood that improvement was a journey, and setbacks were a natural part of the process.

<u>Resilience Beyond Basketball:</u> The resilience the Kings developed extended beyond the basketball court. They applied the same principles to their academic, personal, and

professional lives, becoming well-rounded and resilient individuals.

<u>Overcoming Off-Court Challenges:</u> The Kings faced challenges beyond basketball, such as personal struggles or community issues. Their resilience allowed them to face these challenges head-on and find ways to contribute positively.

<u>Inspiring Others:</u> The power of resilience within the Kings inspired other athletes and members of the community to develop their own resilience. Through their actions, the Kings showed that setbacks did not define one's destiny, but how they bounced back did.

As the East Texas Kings Basketball Program, LLC continued to harness the power of resilience, they knew that it would remain a vital asset in their journey. The heart of a champion knew that true strength came not from avoiding difficulties but from rising above them with unwavering determination.

And so, with hearts full of gratitude, determination, and the power of resilience, the East Texas Kings Basketball Program LLC continued to march forward, forever leaving their mark on the world, one inspired and empowered athlete at a time. For the heart of a champion knows that resilience is not just about winning games; it is about overcoming obstacles, empowering others, and leaving a lasting legacy of strength and perseverance.

Chapter Twenty-Two: Expanding Horizons

As the East Texas Kings Basketball Program, LLC continued their journey, they recognized the importance of expanding their horizons beyond their local community. While their impact had already reached far and wide, they aspired to extend their reach and inspire young athletes beyond their state and even their country's borders.

National Exposure: The Kings sought opportunities to participate in national tournaments and showcase their talent on a broader stage. Competing against teams from different regions allowed them to learn from diverse playing styles and broaden their basketball knowledge.

International Exchange Programs: The Kings explored international exchange programs that would provide their players with the chance to travel and compete overseas. Interacting with athletes from different cultures enriched their understanding of the global basketball community.

Digital Outreach: Leveraging technology, the Kings engaged in digital outreach programs. They connected with aspiring athletes through online clinics, webinars, and social media platforms, providing guidance and inspiration to young players worldwide.

Scholarship Programs: The Kings expanded their scholarship programs, offering opportunities to talented athletes from different states and countries. This initiative aimed to create a diverse and inclusive community of athletes pursuing their dreams together.

Hosting International Events: The Kings considered hosting international basketball events, inviting teams from other countries to compete in their hometown. This not only showcased their community but also fostered cross-cultural exchanges.

Collaborating with International Organizations: The Kings formed partnerships with international sports organizations that shared their vision for empowering young athletes. Through collaborations, they could collectively make a more significant impact on a global scale.

Community Outreach Abroad: The Kings engaged in community outreach projects abroad, bringing their dedication to service to different corners of the world. They collaborated with local organizations to address pressing needs in disadvantaged communities.

<u>Global Philanthropy:</u> The Kings expanded their philanthropic efforts to support causes beyond their local community. They contributed to international projects that aligned with their mission of empowering youth and creating positive change.

<u>Celebrating Diversity:</u> The Kings embraced diversity in all aspects of their program. They welcomed players and coaches from different backgrounds, recognizing the value of diverse perspectives and experiences.

<u>Becoming Global Ambassadors:</u> The Kings saw themselves as global ambassadors for their sport and the values they represented. They understood that their actions, both on and off the court, could inspire and uplift young athletes worldwide.

As the East Texas Kings Basketball Program, LLC expanded their horizons, they knew that the heart of a champion knew no borders. Their impact extended far beyond their local community, touching the lives of aspiring athletes across the globe. They remained committed to empowering the next generation, instilling the values of unity, resilience, and community engagement in young athletes worldwide.

And so, with hearts full of gratitude, determination, and the spirit of global outreach, the East Texas Kings Basketball Program LLC continued to march forward, forever leaving their mark on the world, one inspired and empowered athlete at a time. For the heart of a champion knows that the journey transcends boundaries, embracing diversity, and creating a legacy that spans continents and generations.

Chapter Twenty-Three: Embracing Diversity

Embracing diversity was a fundamental pillar of the East Texas Kings Basketball Program, LLC. Throughout their journey, they recognized that diversity brought strength, unity, and a deeper understanding of the world around them. The Kings celebrated the unique qualities and backgrounds of their players and coaches, fostering an inclusive and supportive environment for all.

Diversity in Recruitment: The Kings actively sought out players and coaches from diverse backgrounds and experiences. They understood that diversity enriched their program, bringing different perspectives and skills to the team.

Building a Multicultural Team: The Kings' roster was a reflection of the diverse community they represented. Players from various ethnicities, cultures, and nationalities came together as one united team, bound by a shared passion for basketball.

Celebrating Differences: The Kings celebrated the differences among their players and coaches, recognizing that each individual's unique attributes contributed to the team's collective strength.

Promoting Inclusivity: The Kings fostered an environment of inclusivity, where everyone felt welcome and valued. They ensured that no one felt like an outsider and that every member of the team had a sense of belonging.

Learning from Each Other: The diverse backgrounds within the Kings provided an opportunity for players and coaches to learn from one another. Cultural exchanges and sharing experiences enhanced the team's camaraderie.

Addressing Biases and Prejudices: The Kings were committed to addressing biases and prejudices within their community and beyond. They actively promoted understanding, empathy, and respect for each other.

Embracing Multilingualism: The Kings embraced multilingualism, recognizing that communication in different languages could foster a more inclusive and connected team dynamic.

Using Diversity as a Strength: The Kings harnessed the power of diversity to create a dynamic playing style and adaptability on the court. They recognized that embracing diverse playing styles led to a more versatile team.

Promoting Diversity Beyond Basketball: The Kings extended their commitment to diversity beyond basketball. They advocated for inclusivity in the community and supported initiatives that promoted diversity and equality.

Becoming Advocates: The Kings saw themselves as advocates for diversity, using their platform to champion the importance of embracing differences and creating a more inclusive world.

As the East Texas Kings Basketball Program, LLC embraced diversity, they knew that the heart of a champion was not confined by boundaries but thrived in the spirit of unity and inclusivity. Their journey was a testament to the transformative power of embracing diversity, not only within the team but in the broader community they served.

And so, with hearts full of gratitude, determination, and the celebration of diversity, the East Texas Kings Basketball Program LLC continued to march forward, forever leaving their mark on the world, one inspired and empowered athlete at a time. For the heart of a champion knows that true strength comes from unity in diversity, creating a legacy of acceptance, respect, and a shared love for the game.

Chapter Twenty-Four: The Impact of Coaching

The impact of coaching was at the core of the East Texas Kings Basketball Program, LLC's success. Throughout their journey, the influence of Coach Justiss Hill and the coaching staff went far beyond the Xs and Os of the game. Their leadership, mentorship, and dedication played a pivotal role in shaping the lives of the players and the program's overall legacy.

Cultivating Leadership: Coach Thompson and the coaching staff focused on developing leadership qualities in the players. They encouraged players to take ownership of their roles, communicate effectively, and lead by example both on and off the court.

Fostering Personal Growth: The coaches prioritized the personal growth and character development of each player. They nurtured qualities such as resilience, self-discipline, and humility, knowing that these traits were equally important as basketball skills.

Individualized Coaching: The Kings' coaching staff recognized the unique strengths and weaknesses of each player. They provided individualized attention and coaching to help players maximize their potential.

Building Trust: Trust was the foundation of the relationship between the coaches and the players. The players trusted the coaching staff to guide them in their development, and the coaches trusted the players to execute their strategies.

Instilling a Winning Culture: Coach Thompson and the coaching staff instilled a winning culture within the Kings. They emphasized the value of hard work, commitment, and the pursuit of excellence, both on and off the court.

Nurturing Team Chemistry: The coaches understood the importance of team chemistry. They organized team-building activities and fostered a positive team culture that encouraged camaraderie and mutual support.

Providing Emotional Support: Beyond basketball, the coaches provided emotional support to the players. They were there to lend a listening ear, offer encouragement during difficult times, and celebrate the players' successes.

Setting High Expectations: The coaching staff set high expectations for the players, challenging them to continually improve and strive for greatness. The belief in their players' potential motivated them to reach new heights.

<u>Modeling Sportsmanship:</u> Coach Thompson and the coaching staff modeled sportsmanship and professionalism. They emphasized the importance of respecting opponents, officials, and the game itself.

<u>Leaving a Lasting Legacy:</u> The impact of coaching extended far beyond a single season. Coach Hill's leadership and the coaching staff's dedication left a lasting legacy on the program and the players' lives.

As the East Texas Kings Basketball Program LLC continued to thrive, they knew that the heart of a champion was built on the foundation of exceptional coaching. The impact of coaching went beyond wins and losses; it was about shaping young athletes into well-rounded, confident individuals who would carry the values instilled in them throughout their lives.

And so, with hearts full of gratitude, determination, and the impact of coaching, the East Texas Kings Basketball Program LLC continued to march forward, forever leaving their mark on the world, one inspired and empowered athlete at a time. For the heart of a champion beats not only on the court but also in the lasting influence of the coaches who guide them toward greatness.

Chapter Twenty-Five:

Giving Back To The Community

As the East Texas Kings Basketball Program LLC achieved success and grew in stature, they never forgot the importance of giving back to their community. The spirit of service and gratitude was ingrained in their culture, and they actively sought ways to make a positive impact on the lives of others.

Community Outreach Programs: The Kings organized community outreach programs, collaborating with local organizations to address pressing issues in their area. They participated in initiatives such as food drives, youth mentoring programs, and educational workshops.

Inspiring the Youth: The Kings understood the power of being role models for young athletes. They visited schools and community centers, sharing their experiences and encouraging the next generation to pursue their dreams with determination.

Basketball Clinics and Camps: The Kings organized basketball clinics and camps, providing aspiring athletes with the opportunity to learn from seasoned players and coaches. These events were often open to the community, promoting the sport and its values.

Supporting Underprivileged Youth: The Kings supported underprivileged youth by providing scholarships, basketball equipment, and other resources necessary to participate in the sport. They wanted to ensure that financial barriers did not limit anyone's access to basketball.

Engaging with Local Causes: The Kings aligned themselves with local causes and events that aimed to make a positive impact. Whether it was participating in charity runs or supporting fundraising efforts, they were actively involved in making a difference.

Community Service Days: The Kings designated community service days where players, coaches, and staff came together to volunteer for various projects. They recognized the importance of giving their time and effort to uplift their community.

Promoting Health and Wellness: The Kings promoted health and wellness in their community by hosting fitness workshops, nutrition seminars, and encouraging an active lifestyle among residents.

<u>Collaborating with Local Businesses:</u> The Kings collaborated with local businesses that shared their commitment to community service. Together, they organized events and programs that benefited the community at large.

<u>Listening to Community Needs:</u> The Kings actively listened to the needs and concerns of their community. They proactively sought feedback and suggestions to ensure that their service efforts were meaningful and effective.

<u>Leaving a Lasting Legacy:</u> The Kings aimed to leave a lasting legacy of giving back. They hoped that their commitment to community service would inspire future generations of athletes to use their platform to create positive change.

As the East Texas Kings Basketball Program, LLC continued to give back to their community, they knew that the heart of a champion extended beyond the basketball court. Their commitment to service and making a difference was a testament to their character and the values they upheld.

And so, with hearts full of gratitude, determination, and the spirit of giving back, the East Texas Kings Basketball Program, LLC continued to march forward, forever leaving their mark on the world, one inspired and empowered athlete at a time. For the heart of a champion knows that true greatness lies not just in victories, but in the positive impact they have on the lives of others and their community.

Chapter Twenty-Six: Navigating Expectations

As the East Texas Kings Basketball Program, LLC continued to achieve success and gain recognition, they faced an increased level of expectations from their community, fans, and even themselves. Navigating these expectations became an essential aspect of their journey, ensuring that they remained grounded and focused on their mission.

Setting Realistic Goals: The Kings set realistic and achievable goals for themselves. While they aimed for success, they understood that it required dedication, hard work, and patience.

Emphasizing the Process: Coach Justiss Hill emphasized the importance of focusing on the process rather than solely fixating on outcomes. The Kings understood that continuous improvement and learning were more valuable than immediate results.

Managing External Pressure: As expectations rose, the Kings learned to manage external pressure. They remained focused on their strengths and values, tuning out distractions and external opinions.

Communicating Openly: The coaching staff encouraged open communication with the players. They discussed the expectations and challenges they faced, fostering an environment where concerns and emotions were acknowledged.

Supporting Each Other: The Kings supported each other during challenging times, knowing that they were in it together. This camaraderie helped them navigate the ups and downs of their journey.

Staying Humble: Despite their successes, the Kings remained humble. They understood that humility was essential in keeping them grounded and maintaining a strong team dynamic.

Learning from Setbacks: Navigating expectations involved learning from setbacks and using them as opportunities for growth. The Kings saw setbacks as a chance to regroup and come back stronger.

Celebrating Progress: The Kings celebrated their progress and achievements along the way. Acknowledging their growth helped boost morale and kept them motivated.

Avoiding Comparison: The Kings avoided comparing themselves to others. They focused on their journey and appreciated the uniqueness of their own path.

Staying True to Their Mission: The Kings always remained true to their mission and values. They understood that success was not solely defined by wins and losses, but by the positive impact they made on and off the court.

As the East Texas Kings Basketball Program, LLC navigated expectations, they knew that the heart of a champion lies in remaining true to their purpose. Their journey was a testament to the strength of character and resilience required to maintain a sense of purpose and perspective amidst increasing expectations.

And so, with hearts full of gratitude, determination, and the wisdom of navigating expectations, the East Texas Kings Basketball Program LLC continued to march forward, forever leaving their mark on the world, one inspired and empowered athlete at a time. For the heart of a champion knows that staying true to oneself is the key to navigating expectations and leaving a lasting legacy of greatness.

From Underdogs To Champions

Chapter Twenty-Seven: The Pursuit of Excellence

The pursuit of excellence was at the core of the East Texas Kings Basketball Program LLC's journey. From the very beginning, they embraced the belief that greatness was not a destination but a continuous journey of improvement and growth. The Kings were committed to pushing their limits and striving for excellence in every aspect of their lives.

Embracing a Growth Mindset: The Kings embraced a growth mindset, believing that their abilities and talents could be developed through hard work and dedication. They viewed challenges as opportunities for learning and improvement.

Investing in Training and Development: The Kings invested in training and development to continually enhance their basketball skills. They understood that consistent practice and coaching were essential for reaching new heights.

Pursuing Mental Excellence: The Kings recognized the importance of mental excellence. They practiced mindfulness, visualization, and mental resilience techniques to strengthen their focus and composure on the court.

Learning from the Best: The Kings sought inspiration from successful athletes and teams, both in basketball and other sports. They studied the strategies and work ethic of champions, applying those lessons to their own pursuit of excellence.

Pushing Beyond Comfort Zones: The Kings understood that growth occurred outside of their comfort zones. They willingly took on new challenges, pushing their limits to discover their true potential.

Celebrating Small Victories: The Kings celebrated the small victories along their journey. Whether it was mastering a new skill or overcoming a personal obstacle, they acknowledged and appreciated each step forward.

Encouraging Healthy Competition: Within the team, healthy competition fostered a culture of excellence. Players pushed each other to improve, raising the overall level of performance.

Analyzing Performance: The Kings meticulously analyzed their performance in games and practices. They used data and feedback to identify areas for improvement and worked tirelessly to address them.

Holding Each Other Accountable: The Kings held each other accountable to their commitments and goals. They knew that excellence required collective effort and support.

Balancing Success and Humility: As the Kings achieved success, they remained humble and focused on continuous improvement. They understood that humility was an essential aspect of the pursuit of excellence.

As the East Texas Kings Basketball Program, LLC continued their pursuit of excellence, they knew that the heart of a champion lay in the relentless commitment to being the best version of themselves. Their journey was a testament to the transformative power of striving for greatness and inspiring others to do the same.

And so, with hearts full of gratitude, determination, and the pursuit of excellence, the East Texas Kings Basketball Program, LLC continued to march forward, forever leaving their mark on the world, one inspired and empowered athlete at a time. For the heart of a champion knows that true greatness is found not only in the destination but in the unwavering pursuit of excellence along the way.

From Underdogs To Champions

Chapter Twenty-Eight: The Power of Visualization

In their quest for excellence, the East Texas Kings Basketball Program, LLC harnessed the power of visualization. They understood that success on the court was not only about physical prowess but also about mental preparation and focus. Visualization became a powerful tool in helping the players elevate their performance and achieve their goals.

Mental Rehearsal: The Kings engaged in mental rehearsal before games and crucial moments. They vividly imagined themselves executing plays, making successful shots, and outperforming their opponents.

Building Confidence: Visualization boosted the players' confidence by instilling a belief in their abilities. They saw themselves succeeding in their mind's eye, which translated to increased self-assurance on the court.

Overcoming Challenges: Through visualization, the Kings mentally prepared for potential challenges and obstacles they might encounter during games. They practiced overcoming these hurdles in their minds, making them better equipped to handle them in reality.

Focusing on Game Strategy: Visualization helped the players internalize the team's game strategy. They mentally walked through various scenarios, enabling them to respond quickly and decisively during actual gameplay.

Enhancing Muscle Memory: Visualizing movements and plays contributed to enhancing muscle memory. When it came time to execute on the court, the players' bodies were primed to perform the actions they had visualized.

Managing Pressure: Visualization helped the players manage pressure and anxiety. By mentally rehearsing success, they reduced performance anxiety and remained focused under high-pressure situations.

Setting Goals: The Kings used visualization to set clear and specific goals for themselves. They visualized achieving these goals, making them more attainable and motivating.

Reviewing Past Performances: The Kings used visualization to review and learn from their past performances. They identified areas for improvement and mentally practiced executing better plays.

Building Team Cohesion: Visualization was not limited to individual players; the Kings used group visualization to strengthen team cohesion. They visualized themselves working cohesively as a unit, building trust and chemistry.

<u>Visualizing Success Beyond Basketball:</u> The power of visualization extended beyond basketball. The Kings used it to visualize success in their academic pursuits, personal goals, and community impact.

As the East Texas Kings Basketball Program, LLC continued to harness the power of visualization, they knew that the heart of a champion beat not only with physical prowess but with mental fortitude. Their journey was a testament to the transformative power of visualization, empowering them to achieve greatness on and off the court.

And so, with hearts full of gratitude, determination, and the power of visualization, the East Texas Kings Basketball Program, LLC continued to march forward, forever leaving their mark on the world, one inspired and empowered athlete at a time. For the heart of a champion knows that success is first envisioned in the mind before it becomes a reality on the court.

From Underdogs To Champions

Chapter Twenty-Nine:

Celebrating Individual Achievements

Within the East Texas Kings Basketball Program, LLC, celebrating individual achievements was an essential part of their team culture. While they emphasized the importance of collective success, they also recognized and acknowledged the unique contributions of each player. The Kings believed that celebrating individual achievements not only boosted morale but also inspired others to strive for greatness.

Player of the Game Recognition: After each game, the Kings celebrated a "Player of the Game." This acknowledgment highlighted the outstanding performance of a player who made a significant impact on the game.

Highlighting Personal Milestones: The Kings recognized and celebrated personal milestones achieved by players, such as scoring milestones, career highs, or exceptional performances.

Weekly Awards: The team organized weekly awards, showcasing various achievements, such as most improved player, best defender, and top rebounder. These awards motivated players to excel in different aspects of the game.

Celebrating Growth and Progress: The Kings celebrated the growth and progress of each player, regardless of their skill level. Improvement and effort were valued and commended.

Honoring Sportsmanship: The Kings acknowledged players who demonstrated outstanding sportsmanship and leadership on and off the court. Their exemplary behavior was recognized and appreciated.

Academic Achievements: The program celebrated academic achievements, such as academic honors or improved grades. They encouraged a well-rounded focus on both academics and athletics.

Community Impact: Individual achievements in community service and outreach were celebrated, as the Kings recognized the value of making a positive impact beyond basketball.

Player Spotlights: The Kings regularly featured player spotlights, where players shared their stories, experiences, and achievements. This highlighted their unique journeys and inspired others.

<u>Supportive Atmosphere:</u> The Kings created a supportive atmosphere where players encouraged and celebrated each other's successes. They understood that lifting each other up fostered a stronger team dynamic.

<u>Recognizing Effort:</u> The Kings acknowledged and celebrated players' efforts, even when the desired outcome was not achieved. Recognizing hard work and dedication motivated players to continue giving their best.

As the East Texas Kings Basketball Program, LLC celebrated individual achievements, they knew that the heart of a champion was not just about winning games, but also about recognizing and appreciating the efforts and accomplishments of every team member. Their journey was a testament to the power of encouragement and positive reinforcement in cultivating a culture of excellence.

And so, with hearts full of gratitude, determination, and the celebration of individual achievements, the East Texas Kings Basketball Program, LLC continued to march forward, forever leaving their mark on the world, one inspired and empowered athlete at a time. For the heart of a champion knows that recognizing and celebrating each player's unique journey is the key to fostering a unified and victorious team.

Chapter Thirty: Embracing Adversity

In the annals of the East Texas Kings Basketball Program, LLC's journey from underdogs to champions, Chapter Thirty revealed a pivotal theme that defined their rise: the art of embracing adversity. It was during moments of challenge that the true character of the team shone through, transforming setbacks into stepping stones toward greatness.

Resilience in Defeat: Adversity wasn't an enemy; it was a teacher. The Kings understood that defeat was an integral part of the journey, offering valuable lessons that could propel them forward. Instead of succumbing to defeat, they used it as a catalyst for growth.

Mental Toughness: The champions weren't immune to doubt and frustration, but they cultivated mental toughness that helped them weather the storms. They harnessed the power of a strong mindset to navigate obstacles with clarity and determination.

Turning Setbacks into Opportunities: Each setback was an opportunity in disguise. The Kings looked beyond immediate losses, analyzing their performance and strategy, and using setbacks as a blueprint for improvement.

Learning from Mistakes: Adversity was the crucible where mistakes were forged into wisdom. The Kings acknowledged their missteps, dissected them, and turned them into valuable learning experiences that fortified their journey.

Unity in Challenges: Adversity had the potential to fracture a team, but the Kings defied this norm. Challenges brought them closer, fostering unity, camaraderie, and an unbreakable bond that carried them through the toughest of times.

Fueling the Fire: Adversity wasn't a deterrent; it was fuel for their fire. The Kings channeled their frustrations into motivation, using the memory of setbacks to propel themselves towards victory.

Overcoming Self-Doubt: Adversity often came hand in hand with self-doubt. The champions learned to silence the whispers of uncertainty and turn them into a rallying cry of determination.

Adapting to Change: The journey from underdogs to champions was a dynamic process. Adversity forced the Kings to adapt, evolve, and uncover innovative solutions that elevated their game.

Celebrating Small Wins: Amidst adversity, the Kings celebrated the small victories that often went unnoticed. These victories were a testament to their resilience and a reminder that progress was being made.

Embracing the Unknown: The champions embraced the uncertainty that adversity brought. They stepped into the unknown with courage, trusting in their preparation and their ability to overcome any challenge.

Heart of a Champion: Through embracing adversity, the heart of a champion beat stronger within the Kings. They understood that true champions weren't defined solely by their victories but by their ability to rise after every fall.

As Chapter Thirty unfolded, the East Texas Kings Basketball Program, LLC continued their transformative journey. Adversity, once seen as a barrier, had become a stepping stone. The champions' ability to face challenges head-on, to transform setbacks into opportunities, and to cultivate resilience set the stage for their ascent to even greater heights.

And so, with hearts full of determination, unity, and the spirit of champions, the Kings continued to march forward, ready to overcome any adversity that came their way.

Chapter Thirty-One: The Spirit of Perseverance

In their pursuit of excellence, the East Texas Kings Basketball Program, LLC embodied the spirit of perseverance. Throughout their journey, they faced numerous challenges and obstacles that tested their resolve. But, like true champions, the Kings never backed down; they embraced adversity with unwavering determination, knowing that their willingness to persevere would lead them to greater heights.

Resilience in Defeat: The Kings understood that defeat was a part of the game. Instead of being disheartened by losses, they used them as fuel to work harder and improve their performance.

Bouncing Back from Setbacks: Injuries and setbacks were not seen as roadblocks, but as opportunities to grow stronger. The Kings showed remarkable resilience, pushing through adversity to come back even stronger.

Embracing Challenges: The Kings didn't shy away from challenging opponents or tough matchups. They welcomed these tests as opportunities to prove their mettle and push their boundaries.

Perseverance in Practice: Every practice was an opportunity to hone their skills and work on weaknesses. The Kings approached each training session with a tenacious desire to improve, never settling for mediocrity.

Mental Fortitude: The Kings developed mental fortitude to stay composed and focused during high-pressure situations. They remained level-headed, trusting in their abilities and staying committed to their game plan.

Turning Failure into Learning: The Kings saw failure as a chance to learn and grow. They analyzed their mistakes, identified areas for improvement, and used these lessons to become better players and a stronger team.

Supporting Each Other: During challenging times, the Kings came together as a united front. They lifted each other up, offering encouragement and support, knowing that they were stronger together.

Staying Committed to the Vision: The Kings remained committed to their vision of excellence, no matter how tough the journey became. They knew that perseverance was the key to achieving their long-term goals.

<u>Celebrating Progress:</u> Even in the face of challenges, the Kings celebrated their progress and the small victories along the way. They acknowledged the hard work and effort put in by each player.

<u>Inspiring Others:</u> The spirit of perseverance within the Kings inspired not only their teammates but also their fans and the entire community. Their determination to never give up became a rallying cry for others facing their own challenges.

As the East Texas Kings Basketball Program, LLC embodied the spirit of perseverance, they knew that the heart of a champion beat not only during moments of triumph but during the moments of struggle and resilience. Their journey was a testament to the transformative power of perseverance, proving that champions were not made overnight but forged through the fire of unwavering determination.

And so, with hearts full of gratitude, determination, and the spirit of perseverance, the East Texas Kings Basketball Program, LLC continued to march forward, forever leaving their mark on the world, one inspired and empowered athlete at a time. For the heart of a champion knows that the road to greatness is paved with perseverance, and every step forward, no matter how small, leads to victory.

Chapter Thirty-Two: The Impact of Mentorship

The East Texas Kings Basketball Program, LLC recognized the profound impact of mentorship on their journey to greatness. Throughout their careers, the players and coaches alike experienced the transformative power of guidance, support, and wisdom from mentors. Mentorship was a cornerstone of their success, shaping not only their basketball skills but also their character and leadership on and off the court.

Guidance and Direction: Mentors provided valuable guidance and direction to the players. They shared their experiences and knowledge, helping the athletes navigate challenges and make informed decisions.

Building Confidence: Through encouragement and constructive feedback, mentors built the players' confidence. They helped the Kings believe in themselves and their abilities, empowering them to reach their full potential.

Cultivating Leadership: Mentors played a pivotal role in cultivating leadership qualities within the players. They nurtured skills such as communication, empathy, and decision-making, fostering a new generation of leaders.

Fostering a Growth Mindset: Mentors instilled a growth mindset in the players, teaching them to view failures as opportunities for learning and improvement. They encouraged the Kings to embrace challenges with a positive and resilient attitude.

Setting Goals and Accountability: Mentors helped the players set clear and achievable goals, holding them accountable to their commitments. This structured approach motivated the Kings to stay focused on their aspirations.

Providing Emotional Support: Beyond the game, mentors offered emotional support to the players. They were a source of encouragement during tough times, providing a listening ear and empathetic guidance.

Modeling Values: Mentors modeled the values and behaviors they wanted to instill in the players. Their actions served as powerful examples, reinforcing the importance of integrity, sportsmanship, and dedication.

Career and Academic Guidance: Mentors offered career and academic guidance to the players, helping them plan for their future beyond basketball. They emphasized the importance of a well-rounded education and personal growth.

Building Lifelong Connections: The mentorship relationships fostered during their time with the Kings extended beyond the basketball court. Players and coaches formed lifelong connections, creating a supportive network of individuals united by their shared experiences.

Paying It Forward: The impact of mentorship inspired the Kings to pay it forward and become mentors to others. They understood the significance of giving back and passing on the knowledge and support they had received.

As the East Texas Kings Basketball Program, LLC experienced the profound impact of mentorship, they knew that the heart of a champion was not solely built on individual talent but also on the guidance and support of mentors. Their journey was a testament to the transformative power of mentorship, empowering them to become not only outstanding athletes but also compassionate, well-rounded individuals.

And so, with hearts full of gratitude, determination, and the impact of mentorship, the East Texas Kings Basketball Program LLC continued to march forward, forever leaving their mark on the world, one inspired and empowered athlete at a time. For the heart of a champion knows that greatness is not achieved alone but through the influence of caring mentors who believe in their potential.

Chapter Thirty-Three: Cultivating a Winning Mindset

A winning mindset was the driving force behind the East Texas Kings Basketball Program, LLC's success. They understood that true victory started not just on the basketball court, but within their minds. Cultivating a winning mindset was a deliberate and ongoing process that empowered the Kings to conquer challenges, overcome obstacles, and achieve greatness.

Positive Self-Talk: The Kings practiced positive self-talk, replacing self-doubt with affirmations of their abilities and potential. They believed in themselves, knowing that a strong mental attitude was the foundation of success.

Visualization of Success: Before each game, the Kings visualized success. They imagined executing plays flawlessly, making critical shots, and celebrating victorious moments, manifesting their winning aspirations.

Embracing Challenges: Instead of fearing challenges, the Kings embraced them as opportunities for growth. They saw challenges as stepping stones to becoming better players and a stronger team.

Learning from Setbacks: A winning mindset allowed the Kings to learn from setbacks rather than dwelling on them. They treated failures as valuable lessons, fueling their determination to bounce back stronger.

Focus on the Process: The Kings shifted their focus from the end result to the process of continuous improvement. They understood that consistent effort and dedication would lead to the desired outcomes.

Resilience in Adversity: Cultivating a winning mindset instilled resilience within the Kings. They were unfazed by setbacks, knowing that resilience was the key to turning adversity into triumph.

Belief in Team Success: Each player believed in the collective success of the team. They understood that individual achievements were secondary to the success of the team as a whole.

Trusting in Preparation: The Kings trusted their preparation and training. They knew that their hard work would pay off, and they approached each game with confidence in their abilities.

Staying Present: A winning mindset helped the Kings stay present in the moment. They focused on the task at hand, avoiding distractions and staying fully engaged in the game.

Celebrating Effort: The Kings celebrated not only the final score but also the effort put forth by each player. They valued hard work, determination, and dedication as much as the final outcome.

As the East Texas Kings Basketball Program, LLC cultivated a winning mindset, they knew that the heart of a champion was not determined solely by talent, but by the unwavering belief in their ability to succeed. Their journey was a testament to the transformative power of a winning mindset, propelling them to achieve greatness and leave an indelible mark on the world of basketball.

And so, with hearts full of gratitude, determination, and a winning mindset, the East Texas Kings Basketball Program, LLC continued to march forward, forever leaving their mark on the world, one inspired and empowered athlete at a time. For the heart of a champion knows that victory begins with a winning mindset, and the belief in oneself opens the door to infinite possibilities on the path to greatness.

From Underdogs To Champions

Chapter Thirty-Four: The Joy of Teamwork

The East Texas Kings Basketball Program, LLC cherished the joy of teamwork, recognizing that their collective strength and unity were essential to their success. Throughout their journey, the Kings experienced the profound joy that came from working together, supporting one another, and celebrating shared victories.

Shared Purpose: The Kings embraced a shared purpose that extended beyond individual aspirations. They were united by their love for the game and a commitment to representing their community with pride.

Camaraderie and Friendship: The bonds of camaraderie and friendship within the team were strong. The players were not only teammates but also friends who genuinely cared for and supported each other.

Sacrifice for the Greater Good: The Kings understood the importance of sacrifice for the greater good of the team. They put aside personal agendas, always prioritizing what was best for the collective.

Embracing Roles: Each player embraced their role within the team, recognizing that every role was crucial to achieving success. They valued each other's contributions, no matter how big or small.

Effective Communication: The Kings maintained open and effective communication both on and off the court. They listened to each other, shared ideas, and worked together to execute their game plan.

Celebrating Team Success: The joy of teamwork was amplified when celebrating team successes. They relished in their shared accomplishments, knowing that they achieved greatness together.

Overcoming Challenges as One: When faced with challenges, the Kings stood together as one. They drew strength from their unity, using it to overcome adversity and emerge stronger as a team.

Trust and Support: Trust and support were pillars of the Kings' teamwork. They trusted one another's abilities and provided unwavering support, creating a safe and encouraging environment.

Learning and Growing Together: The joy of teamwork extended to the process of learning and growing together. They understood that improvement was a collective effort, and they pushed each other to reach new heights.

Lifelong Connections: The joy of teamwork forged lifelong connections among the Kings. Even after their playing days, they remained connected by the memories and experiences they shared as a team.

As the East Texas Kings Basketball Program, LLC experienced the joy of teamwork, they knew that the heart of a champion beat not just as individuals but as a united force. Their journey was a testament to the transformative power of teamwork, reminding them that the true essence of victory lies in the bonds they forged and the collective joy they experienced on the court.

And so, with hearts full of gratitude, determination, and the joy of teamwork, the East Texas Kings Basketball Program, LLC continued to march forward, forever leaving their mark on the world, one inspired and empowered athlete at a time. For the heart of a champion knows that together, they are unstoppable, and the joy of teamwork is the true essence of victory.

Chapter Thirty-Five: Leaving a Legacy

As the East Texas Kings Basketball Program, LLC's journey continued, they were mindful of the legacy they were building. They knew that their impact extended far beyond the basketball court and that their actions would leave a lasting impression on their community and future generations of athletes.

Inspiring the Next Generation: The Kings understood the responsibility they had as role models for young athletes. They aimed to inspire the next generation to pursue their dreams with dedication and integrity.

Empowering Through Community Service: Leaving a legacy meant making a positive impact beyond basketball. The Kings continued their community service efforts, empowering and uplifting those in need.

Upholding Values: The Kings upheld their core values of sportsmanship, teamwork, and perseverance. They instilled these values not only in their players but also in the broader community.

Creating a Strong Team Culture: The Kings cultivated a strong team culture of unity, support, and excellence. This culture became the foundation for future teams and players who would carry on the legacy.

Supporting Local Youth Programs: The Kings actively supported local youth basketball programs and initiatives. They invested in the development of young athletes, nurturing their passion for the sport.

Giving Back to Their Alma Mater: Many of the Kings graduated from local schools, and they gave back by supporting their alma maters' sports programs and academic initiatives.

Mentoring and Coaching: The Kings became mentors and coaches to aspiring athletes, passing on their knowledge and experiences. They contributed to the growth and success of future basketball stars.

Creating Lasting Memories: Through their achievements, the Kings created lasting memories for their fans and community. Their triumphs on the court became an integral part of the area's sports history.

Being Involved in the Community: The Kings remained involved in community events, fundraisers, and charity drives. Their presence and support strengthened the bond between the team and the community.

<u>Embodying Sportsmanship and Respect:</u> Above all, the Kings left a legacy of sportsmanship and respect. They demonstrated the highest level of integrity both in victory and defeat, leaving a positive impression on all who encountered them.

As the East Texas Kings Basketball Program, LLC strived to leave a legacy, they knew that the heart of a champion was not measured by individual accolades, but by the positive impact they made on their community and the lives they touched. Their journey was a testament to the transformative power of leaving a legacy that transcends the boundaries of the game and echoes for generations to come.

And so, with hearts full of gratitude, determination, and the desire to leave a lasting legacy, the East Texas Kings Basketball Program, LLC continued to march forward, forever leaving their mark on the world, one inspired and empowered athlete at a time. For the heart of a champion knows that the legacy they leave behind is a testament to their greatness and the positive change they created in the world.

Chapter 36:
The Memorial Service of a Fallen Teammate

In the midst of their journey from underdogs to champions, the East Texas Kings faced a devastating loss that shook the entire team to its core. One of their beloved teammates, Douglas, tragically passed away in a hit and run car accident. The news sent shockwaves through the community, leaving the Kings and their supporters heartbroken.

As the team mourned the loss of their fallen teammate, they realized that they needed to come together not only to honor Douglas' memory but also to find strength in each other. They decided to hold a memorial service to celebrate Douglas' life and the impact he had on their team.

The memorial service took place in the gymnasium where the Kings had spent countless hours practicing and playing together. The space was transformed into a place of remembrance, adorned with photos of Douglas, his basketball jersey, and messages of love and support from the community.

The entire community came together to pay their respects. Douglas' family, friends, teammates, coaches, and even rival teams attended the service. The gymnasium was filled with tears, hugs, and shared memories of Douglas Reed's infectious smile, his passion for the game, and his unwavering dedication to his teammates.

Coach Hill, his voice filled with emotion, spoke about Douglas' impact on the team. He shared stories of Douglas' leadership, his selflessness, and his ability to bring out the best in his teammates. Coach Hill emphasized that Douglas' spirit would continue to guide and inspire the Kings as they moved forward.

Each member of the team took turns sharing their own memories and reflections. They spoke of Douglas' encouragement during tough practices, his ability to lift their spirits when they were down, and his unwavering belief in their abilities. Through tears and laughter, they celebrated the bond they had formed with Douglas and vowed to honor his memory by giving their all on and off the court.

The memorial service ended with a moment of silence, followed by a standing ovation that echoed throughout the gymnasium. The Kings, their heads held high, walked out of the gymnasium with a renewed sense of purpose. They knew that Douglas would be with them every step of the way as they continued their journey from underdogs to champions.

In the days and weeks that followed, the Kings channeled their grief into their training and games. They played with a fire and determination that was unmatched. They carried Douglas's memory in their hearts, using it as fuel to push themselves to new heights.

From Underdogs To Champions

Chapter Thirty-Seven: Beyond Boundaries

As the East Texas Kings Basketball Program, LLC continued their journey, they discovered that the impact of their endeavors extended far beyond their local community. The power of basketball transcended geographical boundaries, connecting them with athletes, fans, and communities from different cultures and backgrounds. Embracing this global reach, the Kings found new opportunities to make a positive impact and spread their message of unity and excellence.

International Friendships: Through tournaments and exchanges, the Kings formed international friendships with athletes from various countries. They celebrated the diversity of cultures, languages, and traditions that basketball brought together.

Cultural Exchange: The Kings engaged in cultural exchange, learning about the customs and traditions of other communities. They shared their own experiences, fostering a mutual understanding and appreciation of diversity.

Empowering Young Athletes Globally: The Kings recognized their role as global ambassadors for the sport.

They sought to inspire and empower young athletes worldwide, encouraging them to pursue their dreams fearlessly.

Raising Awareness for Causes: The Kings utilized their global platform to raise awareness for causes they believed in, such as social justice, education, and environmental sustainability.

Collaborating with International Organizations: The Kings collaborated with international organizations dedicated to sports development and social impact. They worked hand-in-hand to drive positive change on a global scale.

Showcasing Unity Through Sports: The Kings used sports as a vehicle to showcase the power of unity and collaboration. They demonstrated that despite differences, a shared love for the game could unite people from all walks of life.

Representing Their Community Proudly: As they traveled the world, the Kings proudly represented their community and its values. They became ambassadors not only for their sport but also for the principles they stood for.

Inspiring Future Global Leaders: The Kings aspired to inspire future global leaders who would use sports as a tool for positive change and bring people together across borders.

Spreading Messages of Positivity: The Kings spread messages of positivity, hope, and perseverance through their interactions with international audiences. They aimed to uplift and encourage those they encountered.

Making a Lasting Impact: Beyond the boundaries of their local courts, the Kings sought to make a lasting impact on a global scale, leaving a positive legacy that transcended borders and time.

As the East Texas Kings Basketball Program, LLC embraced the power of basketball beyond boundaries, they knew that the heart of a champion was not confined to a specific location but had the potential to touch lives across the world. Their journey was a testament to the transformative power of sports as a universal language, fostering connections and creating positive change on a global level.

And so, with hearts full of gratitude, determination, and the spirit of global impact, the East Texas Kings Basketball Program, LLC continued to march forward, forever leaving their mark on the world, one inspired and empowered athlete at a time. For the heart of a champion knows that the power of basketball knows no borders, and through the game, they can unite the world in the pursuit of a brighter future.

Chapter Thirty-Eight: The Heart of Service

The East Texas Kings Basketball Program, LLC understood the profound impact of service to others. They recognized that true greatness extended beyond the basketball court and into the lives of those in need. The heart of service was at the core of their journey, driving them to give back, uplift their community, and make a positive difference in the world.

Community Outreach: The Kings actively engaged in community outreach, organizing events and initiatives to support local causes and those less fortunate.

Volunteering: They volunteered their time and skills to help various charitable organizations and community projects, lending a helping hand to those in need.

Empowering Youth: The Kings mentored and inspired local youth, encouraging them to pursue their dreams and providing positive role models for the next generation.

Supporting Education: Education was a priority for the Kings. They supported educational programs and initiatives that aimed to provide better opportunities for young people.

Charitable Fundraisers: The Kings organized charitable fundraisers to raise funds for causes they believed in, turning their basketball events into platforms for positive change.

Spreading Awareness: They used their platform to spread awareness about social issues and encourage others to get involved in making a difference.

Community Cleanups: The Kings participated in community cleanups, taking responsibility for the environment they played in and promoting a cleaner, healthier community.

Inspiring Acts of Kindness: The Kings encouraged acts of kindness among their fans and community, recognizing that even small gestures could have a significant impact.

Partnering with Nonprofits: They partnered with local and national nonprofits to extend their reach and maximize their impact on various causes.

Leaving a Lasting Impact: The heart of service was not a one-time event for the Kings; it was a continuous commitment to making a lasting impact on their community and beyond.

As the East Texas Kings Basketball Program, LLC lived by the heart of service, they knew that the heart of a champion beat not only for personal success but for the betterment of others. Their journey was a testament to the transformative power of service, reminding them that their greatness was measured not just by their achievements on the court but by the positive change they created in the lives of others.

And so, with hearts full of gratitude, determination, and the spirit of service, the East Texas Kings Basketball Program LLC continued to march forward, forever leaving their mark on the world, one inspired and empowered athlete at a time. For the heart of a champion knows that true greatness is achieved through acts of service and the impact they leave on the hearts and lives of others.

From Underdogs To Champions

Chapter Thirty-Nine: Life Lessons from the Game

The game of basketball taught the East Texas Kings Basketball Program, LLC valuable life lessons that extended far beyond the boundaries of the court. Throughout their journey, they embraced these lessons and applied them to their personal and professional lives, enriching their character and shaping their path to success.

Resilience: Basketball taught the Kings the importance of resilience in the face of adversity. They learned to bounce back from setbacks, embracing challenges as opportunities for growth.

Teamwork: The power of teamwork on the basketball court translated into the understanding that collaboration and support were essential in all aspects of life.

Perseverance: The Kings understood that perseverance was the key to achieving their goals. They learned to stay committed and dedicated, even when faced with obstacles.

Sportsmanship: Basketball taught the Kings the value of sportsmanship and fair play. They demonstrated respect for opponents, officials, and teammates alike.

Time Management: Balancing practice, games, and personal commitments taught the Kings valuable time management skills, enabling them to prioritize and stay organized.

Discipline: The demands of training and competition instilled discipline within the Kings. They applied this discipline to their studies, careers, and personal aspirations.

Leadership: As they embraced leadership roles on the team, the Kings developed the qualities of effective leadership, both on and off the court.

Adaptability: The ever-changing nature of the game taught the Kings the importance of adaptability and being open to new strategies and approaches.

Confidence: Success on the basketball court boosted the Kings' confidence, teaching them the importance of believing in their abilities and trusting their instincts.

Gratitude: Basketball instilled a sense of gratitude in the Kings for the opportunities they had and the support they received. They learned to appreciate their blessings and express thanks to those who helped them along the way.

As the East Texas Kings Basketball Program, LLC embraced life lessons from the game, they knew that the heart of a champion was not confined to the basketball court, but echoed through every aspect of their lives. Their journey was a testament to the transformative power of sports in shaping character and cultivating qualities that would serve them well beyond their playing days.

And so, with hearts full of gratitude, determination, and the wisdom of life lessons from the game, the East Texas Kings Basketball Program, LLC continued to march forward, forever leaving their mark on the world, one inspired and empowered athlete at a time. For the heart of a champion knows that the game of basketball teaches more than winning and losing; it teaches the essence of becoming a better human being.

From Underdogs To Champions

Chapter Forty: The Endless Journey

As the East Texas Kings Basketball Program, LLC reflected on their journey, they realized that it was an endless one. There were no final destinations, only new goals and dreams waiting to be achieved. The Kings embraced the joy of the journey and understood that the pursuit of excellence was a lifelong commitment, one that brought fulfillment, growth, and lasting impact in every step they took.

And so, with hearts full of gratitude, determination, and the lessons learned, the East Texas Kings Basketball Program LLC continued to march forward, forever leaving their mark on the world, one inspired and empowered athlete at a time. For the heart of a champion knows that the journey is the destination, and their legacy lives on in the lives they touched and the positive change they created.

From Underdogs To Champions

Chapter Forty-One: The Spirit of Sportsmanship

In the heart of the East Texas Kings Basketball Program, LLC, the spirit of sportsmanship burned brightly. They understood that the game of basketball was not just about competing to win; it was about upholding the values of respect, integrity, and camaraderie both on and off the court.

Respect for Opponents: The Kings treated their opponents with respect, recognizing their hard work and dedication to the game. They displayed graciousness in victory and humility in defeat.

Fair Play: Sportsmanship meant adhering to the rules of the game and playing with fairness and honesty. The Kings believed that a fair competition brought out the best in both teams.

Supporting Teammates: The spirit of sportsmanship was evident in the way the Kings supported and uplifted their teammates. They celebrated each other's successes and provided encouragement during challenging times.

Grace in Victory and Defeat: Whether the Kings emerged victorious or faced a defeat, they showed grace and dignity.

They understood that maintaining composure in both situations was a mark of true sportsmanship.

Encouraging Opponents: The Kings recognized the importance of encouraging their opponents to perform at their best. They praised their competitors' skills and efforts, fostering a positive atmosphere on the court.

Embracing the Spirit of the Game: For the Kings, sportsmanship meant embracing the true spirit of the game. They played with passion, commitment, and a genuine love for basketball.

Building Lasting Connections: Through the spirit of sportsmanship, the Kings built lasting connections with their opponents, coaches, and fans. They understood that basketball was a unifying force that transcended rivalries.

Valuing Off-Court Interactions: Beyond the game, the Kings engaged in friendly interactions with their opponents and supported their basketball endeavors beyond competition.

Leading by Example: The Kings saw themselves as ambassadors of sportsmanship. They aimed to set an example for young athletes, inspiring them to embody the values of respect and fair play.

<u>Embracing the Bigger Picture:</u> The Kings recognized that basketball was just one aspect of life. They understood that the true measure of their character was revealed in how they treated others both on and off the court.

As the East Texas Kings Basketball Program, LLC upheld the spirit of sportsmanship, they knew that the heart of a champion was not solely determined by victories but by the positive impact they had on the basketball community and beyond. Their journey was a testament to the transformative power of sportsmanship, reminding them that true greatness was found not just in skill and athleticism but in the character and sportsmanship they displayed.

And so, with hearts full of gratitude, determination, and the spirit of sportsmanship, the East Texas Kings Basketball Program, LLC continued to march forward, forever leaving their mark on the world, one inspired and empowered athlete at a time. For the heart of a champion knows that in the pursuit of excellence, the true victory lies in embracing the spirit of sportsmanship and leaving a legacy of respect and integrity for generations to come.

Chapter Forty-Two:

Building Bridges Through Basketball

The East Texas Kings Basketball Program, LLC recognized that basketball had the power to build bridges and bring people together from different backgrounds and communities. They saw the sport as a unifying force that transcended boundaries and fostered connections among diverse individuals.

Inclusive Events and Tournaments: The Kings organized inclusive events and tournaments that welcomed players from various regions, cultures, and skill levels. They aimed to create a platform where everyone felt valued and included.

Cultural Exchanges: Through basketball, the Kings engaged in cultural exchanges with teams from different cities, states, and even countries. They celebrated the diversity of cultures, learning from one another and building lasting friendships.

Embracing Differences: Basketball taught the Kings to appreciate and embrace the differences among players.

They valued the unique talents and perspectives that each individual brought to the game.

Collaborating with Local Organizations: The Kings collaborated with local community organizations to promote basketball as a means of breaking down barriers and fostering understanding among diverse groups.

Youth Outreach Programs: The Kings established youth outreach programs in underserved communities, using basketball as a tool to inspire and empower young individuals, regardless of their backgrounds.

Unity Through Sports: The Kings believed that sports, especially basketball, had the power to unite people, transcending differences and creating a sense of unity among players and fans alike.

Promoting Peace and Harmony: Through basketball, the Kings promoted peace and harmony, encouraging dialogue and cooperation among communities that may have had historical tensions.

Empowering the Next Generation: The Kings sought to empower the next generation of athletes to use basketball as a vehicle for social change and a tool to bridge divides.

<u>Emphasizing Respect and Sportsmanship:</u> The Kings understood that building bridges required mutual respect and sportsmanship. They exemplified these values, inspiring others to do the same.

<u>Celebrating Global Basketball Culture:</u> Basketball brought together a global community of fans and players. The Kings celebrated the universal love for the game and its ability to connect people worldwide.

As the East Texas Kings Basketball Program, LLC built bridges through basketball, they knew that the heart of a champion beat not just for individual success but for the betterment of the broader community. Their journey was a testament to the transformative power of sports in breaking down barriers, fostering connections, and promoting understanding among diverse individuals.

And so, with hearts full of gratitude, determination, and the spirit of building bridges through basketball, the East Texas Kings Basketball Program, LLC continued to march forward, forever leaving their mark on the world, one inspired and empowered athlete at a time. For the heart of a champion knows that true greatness lies not just in winning games, but in the positive impact they create, building bridges of unity and understanding across the globe.

Chapter Forty-Three: Empowering Women in Sports

The East Texas Kings Basketball Program, LLC recognized the importance of gender equality in sports and were dedicated to empowering women in the world of basketball. They believed that every athlete, regardless of gender, deserved equal opportunities and recognition for their talents and contributions to the game.

Promoting Women's Basketball: The Kings actively promoted women's basketball within their community and beyond. They organized events, tournaments, and showcases that highlighted the talents of female athletes.

Supporting Women's Teams: The Kings supported women's basketball teams in their region by attending their games, offering encouragement, and advocating for equal resources and facilities.

Encouraging Female Participation: The Kings encouraged young girls to participate in basketball by providing mentorship and coaching opportunities. They wanted to instill confidence in female athletes and inspire them to pursue their passion for the game.

Challenging Stereotypes: The Kings worked to challenge stereotypes and perceptions that limited the growth of women in sports. They promoted the idea that women could excel and lead in any field, including basketball.

Equal Training Opportunities: The Kings ensured that female athletes had access to the same high-quality training facilities, coaching, and resources as their male counterparts.

Showcasing Role Models: The Kings celebrated the achievements of female basketball players and coaches who served as role models for aspiring athletes.

Advocating for Fair Compensation: The Kings advocated for fair compensation and recognition for female athletes, seeking to close the gender pay gap in sports.

Addressing Barriers: The Kings addressed any barriers that prevented female athletes from excelling in basketball, working to create an inclusive and supportive environment for all players.

Empowering Female Coaches: The Kings encouraged and supported female coaches in their community, recognizing the importance of diverse leadership in sports.

Leading by Example: Above all, the Kings led by example in empowering women in sports. They demonstrated their commitment to gender equality through their actions and initiatives.

As the East Texas Kings Basketball Program, LLC empowered women in sports, they knew that the heart of a champion was not confined to gender but encompassed the drive to uplift and support all athletes in their pursuit of greatness. Their journey was a testament to the transformative power of promoting inclusivity and equality, reminding them that the true essence of sports lies in embracing and empowering every player, regardless of their gender.

And so, with hearts full of gratitude, determination, and the spirit of empowering women in sports, the East Texas Kings Basketball Program, LLC continued to march forward, forever leaving their mark on the world, one inspired and empowered athlete at a time. For the heart of a champion knows that true greatness is achieved not just by individual accomplishments but by fostering an environment of inclusivity and equality in the sports community.

From Underdogs To Champions

Chapter Forty-Four: The Importance of Mental Health

Within the East Texas Kings Basketball Program, LLC, mental health was a top priority. They understood that a strong and resilient mind was essential for peak performance on the court and in all aspects of life. They actively promoted mental well-being and provided support to ensure that their players and community members were mentally healthy and able to cope with the challenges they faced.

Mental Health Awareness: The Kings actively promoted mental health awareness within their community. They conducted workshops, seminars, and discussions to educate their players and fans about the importance of mental well-being.

Encouraging Open Dialogue: The Kings fostered an environment where individuals felt comfortable discussing their mental health challenges. They encouraged open dialogue and provided a safe space for their players to share their feelings.

Mental Health Resources: The Kings provided access to mental health resources and professionals for their players and community members. They ensured that anyone in need of support could seek help without hesitation.

Stress Management: Stress was a common factor in the competitive world of sports. The Kings taught stress management techniques to their players, helping them cope with pressure in a healthy way.

Mindfulness Training: The Kings incorporated mindfulness training into their practices, helping their players stay present, focused, and mentally resilient during games and in daily life.

Creating a Supportive Environment: The Kings cultivated a supportive and empathetic team environment. They understood that the well-being of their players was just as crucial as their physical fitness.

Addressing Stigma: The Kings worked to break the stigma around mental health, emphasizing that seeking help and support was a sign of strength, not weakness.

Building Resilience: The Kings focused on building mental resilience in their players. They taught them how to bounce back from setbacks and stay mentally strong during challenging times.

<u>Balancing Basketball and Mental Health:</u> The Kings emphasized the importance of balancing basketball commitments with self-care and mental health. They encouraged their players to take breaks and prioritize their well-being.

<u>Long-Term Well-Being:</u> Above all, the Kings recognized that mental health was not just about short-term coping, but about fostering long-term well-being for their players and community.

As the East Texas Kings Basketball Program, LLC emphasized the importance of mental health, they knew that the heart of a champion was not just about physical strength but also about mental fortitude. Their journey was a testament to the transformative power of mental well-being, reminding them that true greatness extended beyond physical skills and accomplishments.

And so, with hearts full of gratitude, determination, and the spirit of mental well-being, the East Texas Kings Basketball Program, LLC continued to march forward, forever leaving their mark on the world, one inspired and empowered athlete at a time. For the heart of a champion knows that true greatness is achieved not only through physical prowess but through mental strength and well-being, ensuring a sustainable journey of success and fulfillment.

Chapter Forty-Five: Mindfulness and Focus

Within the East Texas Kings Basketball Program, LLC, mindfulness and focus were paramount to their success both on and off the court. They recognized that being present in the moment and maintaining unwavering focus were essential for peak performance and achieving their goals.

Mindfulness Training: The Kings incorporated mindfulness training into their daily routines. They practiced techniques such as meditation, deep breathing, and visualization to stay centered and focused.

Being Present in Practice: During practices, the Kings encouraged their players to be fully present and engaged. They emphasized the importance of giving their best effort in every drill and honing their skills with full attention.

Staying in the Zone: The Kings knew that being in the "zone" required complete focus and concentration. They taught their players to block out distractions and maintain mental clarity during games.

Overcoming Pressure: Mindfulness helped the Kings' players handle pressure situations with composure. They learned to embrace challenges and perform at their best even in high-stress moments.

Enhancing Decision-Making: By practicing mindfulness, the Kings improved their players' decision-making abilities. They made calculated choices on the court, leading to more efficient gameplay.

Handling Adversity: Mindfulness taught the Kings' players to handle adversity with grace. They stayed mentally strong during difficult times and used setbacks as opportunities for growth.

Embracing the Present Moment: The Kings understood that focusing on the present moment was crucial for peak performance. They let go of past mistakes and future worries, channeling their energy into the current play.

Mental Preparation: Mindfulness helped the Kings mentally prepare for games and important moments. They visualized success and built confidence in their abilities.

Mind-Body Connection: The Kings recognized the strong connection between the mind and body. They practiced mindfulness to maintain physical and mental balance.

<u>Cultivating Resilience:</u> Mindfulness fostered resilience within the Kings. They rebounded quickly from mistakes and remained determined to improve and succeed.

As the East Texas Kings Basketball Program, LLC embraced mindfulness and focus, they knew that the heart of a champion was not just about physical prowess but about the mental strength to overcome obstacles and perform at their best consistently. Their journey was a testament to the transformative power of mindfulness, reminding them that true greatness was achieved by mastering the art of being fully present and focused in every aspect of their lives.

And so, with hearts full of gratitude, determination, and the spirit of mindfulness and focus, the East Texas Kings Basketball Program, LLC continued to march forward, forever leaving their mark on the world, one inspired and empowered athlete at a time. For the heart of a champion knows that true greatness is not measured solely by victories but by the ability to stay present, focused, and mindful on the journey to success.

From Underdogs To Champions

Chapter Forty-Six: The Impact of Nutrition

The East Texas Kings Basketball Program, LLC understood the significant impact of nutrition on their athletic performance and overall well-being. They recognized that proper nutrition was essential for fueling their bodies, supporting recovery, and optimizing their abilities on the basketball court.

Balanced Diet: The Kings followed a balanced diet that included a variety of nutrients, such as carbohydrates, proteins, fats, vitamins, and minerals. They understood that each nutrient played a vital role in their performance.

Pre-Game Fueling: Before games and practices, the Kings focused on consuming nutritious meals that provided them with sustained energy and stamina throughout the session.

Hydration: Staying hydrated was a priority for the Kings. They drank plenty of water and replenished electrolytes to prevent dehydration during intense training and games.

Recovery Nutrition: After rigorous practices and games, the Kings consumed foods that aided in muscle recovery and repair. They prioritized post-workout meals to optimize their recovery.

Nutrient Timing: The Kings understood the importance of nutrient timing. They consumed specific nutrients before, during, and after workouts to maximize their benefits.

Customized Meal Plans: Some players had specific dietary needs or preferences. The Kings worked with nutritionists to create individualized meal plans tailored to each player's requirements.

Healthy Snacking: The Kings promoted healthy snacking options, ensuring that their players had nutritious choices available between meals to maintain energy levels.

Avoiding Unhealthy Habits: The Kings discouraged unhealthy eating habits, such as excessive consumption of sugary or processed foods, which could negatively impact their performance.

Nutritional Education: The Kings provided their players with nutritional education, empowering them to make informed choices about their diets and lifestyle.

Long-Term Health: Above all, the Kings recognized that proper nutrition was essential for their long-term health and well-being, extending far beyond their basketball careers.

As the East Texas Kings Basketball Program, LLC embraced the impact of nutrition, they knew that the heart of a champion was not just about skill and training, but about taking care of their bodies and nurturing their physical abilities through proper nourishment. Their journey was a testament to the transformative power of nutrition, reminding them that true greatness was achieved not just through talent and hard work but through a holistic approach to health and wellness.

And so, with hearts full of gratitude, determination, and the spirit of embracing the impact of nutrition, the East Texas Kings Basketball Program, LLC continued to march forward, forever leaving their mark on the world, one inspired and empowered athlete at a time. For the heart of a champion knows that true greatness is not only measured by achievements on the court but by the commitment to nourishing the body and mind for sustained excellence in all aspects of life.

From Underdogs To Champions

Chapter Forty-Seven: Embracing Innovation

Innovation was at the core of the East Texas Kings Basketball Program, LLC's journey to success. They recognized that staying ahead in the ever-evolving world of basketball required embracing new ideas, technologies, and strategies to continuously improve their game.

Advanced Training Techniques: The Kings integrated advanced training techniques into their practices. They leveraged modern training equipment and methods to enhance their players' skills and physical conditioning.

Data Analytics: The Kings utilized data analytics to gain insights into player performance and game strategies. They analyzed statistics to make informed decisions and optimize their gameplay.

Sports Science: The Kings incorporated sports science principles into their training regimen. They employed sports physiologists and biomechanics experts to support their players' physical development.

Video Analysis: The Kings used video analysis to review their games and practices. They identified strengths, weaknesses, and areas for improvement, enabling them to refine their approach.

Mental Training Apps: The Kings explored mental training apps and techniques to enhance their players' mental resilience and focus during high-pressure situations.

Virtual Reality Training: The Kings embraced virtual reality training to simulate game scenarios and allow their players to practice in realistic, pressure-filled environments.

Wearable Technology: The Kings equipped their players with wearable technology to track their performance metrics, monitor vital signs, and optimize training and recovery.

Coaching Innovations: The Kings encouraged their coaching staff to embrace innovative coaching techniques. They attended coaching seminars and workshops to stay updated on the latest trends in the game.

Fan Engagement: The Kings leveraged digital platforms and social media to engage with their fans and build a global community around their team.

<u>Constant Adaptation:</u> Above all, the Kings fostered a culture of constant adaptation. They understood that innovation was an ongoing process, and they remained open to new ideas that could propel them to new heights.

As the East Texas Kings Basketball Program, LLC embraced innovation, they knew that the heart of a champion was not just about skill and talent, but about being forward-thinking and adaptable. Their journey was a testament to the transformative power of embracing innovation, reminding them that true greatness was achieved not by resting on past accomplishments but by constantly seeking improvement and embracing change.

And so, with hearts full of gratitude, determination, and the spirit of embracing innovation, the East Texas Kings Basketball Program, LLC continued to march forward, forever leaving their mark on the world, one inspired and empowered athlete at a time. For the heart of a champion knows that true greatness is not only about achieving success but about leading the way in embracing new possibilities and shaping the future of the game.

From Underdogs To Champions

Chapter Forty-Eight: Paying Gratitude Forward

Within the East Texas Kings Basketball Program, LLC, gratitude was not just a feeling but a guiding principle that fueled their actions. They understood that their success was a result of the support and encouragement they received from their community, and they were committed to paying that gratitude forward in meaningful ways.

Community Outreach: The Kings actively engaged in community outreach programs to give back to the people who supported them. They organized charity events, fundraisers, and volunteer activities to support local causes.

Youth Development: The Kings invested in the development of young athletes, providing mentorship, coaching, and resources to aspiring players in their community.

Scholarships and Grants: The Kings established scholarships and grants for promising young basketball players, ensuring that financial constraints would not hinder their dreams.

Supporting Local Businesses: The Kings patronized local businesses and collaborated with them to promote economic growth within their community.

Philanthropic Initiatives: The Kings aligned with philanthropic initiatives and contributed to charitable organizations, amplifying the impact of their giving.

Expressing Gratitude: The Kings took the time to express gratitude to their fans, supporters, and everyone who contributed to their journey. They understood the value of appreciation and reciprocated the love they received.

Inspiring Others: The Kings used their platform to inspire others to pay gratitude forward. They encouraged their fans and fellow athletes to give back to their communities and make a positive impact.

Mentorship Programs: The Kings established mentorship programs that allowed their players and coaches to share their knowledge and experiences with aspiring athletes.

Spreading Positivity: The Kings used their influence to spread positivity and kindness in their community and beyond, creating a ripple effect of gratitude and goodwill.

Leaving a Lasting Legacy: Above all, the Kings aspired to leave a lasting legacy of gratitude and giving back, ensuring that their impact extended far beyond their playing days.

As the East Texas Kings Basketball Program, LLC paid gratitude forward, they knew that the heart of a champion was not just about personal achievements but about lifting others up and creating a positive and supportive community. Their journey was a testament to the transformative power of gratitude, reminding them that true greatness was achieved not just through victories on the court but through the ability to give back and make a difference in the lives of others.

And so, with hearts full of gratitude, determination, and the spirit of paying gratitude forward, the East Texas Kings Basketball Program, LLC continued to march forward, forever leaving their mark on the world, one inspired and empowered athlete at a time. For the heart of a champion knows that true greatness is achieved not just through personal success but through the willingness to extend a hand of gratitude and kindness to others, shaping a better world for all.

From Underdogs To Champions

Chapter Forty-Nine:

Celebrating Diversity and Inclusion

In the heart of the East Texas Kings Basketball Program, LLC, celebrating diversity and inclusion was not just a goal, but a fundamental aspect of their team culture. They believed that embracing diversity enriched their team and community, fostering an environment where everyone felt valued, respected, and empowered.

Embracing Cultural Diversity: The Kings celebrated the cultural diversity of their players and community members. They recognized that different backgrounds brought unique perspectives and talents to the team.

Inclusive Team Environment: The Kings cultivated an inclusive team environment where all players felt welcome and accepted, regardless of their race, ethnicity, gender, or background.

Equal Opportunities: The Kings ensured that all players, regardless of their background, had equal opportunities to showcase their skills and contribute to the team's success.

Respect for Differences: The Kings promoted a culture of respect, encouraging their players to embrace each other's differences and learn from one another.

Anti-Discrimination Policy: The Kings implemented an anti-discrimination policy that prohibited any form of prejudice or bias within their team and organization.

Community Outreach: The Kings engaged in community outreach efforts that reached diverse groups and celebrated the multiculturalism of their community.

Engaging with Diverse Fans: The Kings embraced their diverse fan base and actively engaged with fans from different backgrounds, recognizing the power of sport in bringing people together.

Supporting Inclusive Initiatives: The Kings supported inclusive initiatives and events that celebrated diversity and promoted equality in sports.

Partnering with Diverse Organizations: The Kings partnered with organizations that promoted diversity and inclusion, working together to make a positive impact in their community.

<u>Leading by Example:</u> Above all, the Kings led by example in celebrating diversity and inclusion. They demonstrated through their actions that a united and diverse team could achieve greatness on and off the court.

As the East Texas Kings Basketball Program, LLC celebrated diversity and inclusion, they knew that the heart of a champion was not defined by individual achievements but by the strength of their unity as a diverse team. Their journey was a testament to the transformative power of embracing diversity, reminding them that true greatness was achieved not just through skill and talent but through the ability to come together as one, celebrating the beauty of humanity's differences.

And so, with hearts full of gratitude, determination, and the spirit of celebrating diversity and inclusion, the East Texas Kings Basketball Program, LLC continued to march forward, forever leaving their mark on the world, one inspired and empowered athlete at a time. For the heart of a champion knows that true greatness is not just about winning games but about building a community that cherishes diversity and creates an inclusive space for all to thrive.

From Underdogs To Champions

Chapter Fifty: The Power of Endurance

Endurance was the backbone of the East Texas Kings Basketball Program, LLC's journey to greatness. They understood that success was not achieved overnight, but through perseverance, dedication, and the willingness to keep pushing forward, even in the face of challenges and setbacks.

Resilience in the Face of Adversity: The Kings demonstrated resilience when faced with challenges on and off the court. They refused to give up, learning from their mistakes, and coming back stronger.

Long-Term Vision: The Kings maintained a long-term vision for their success. They understood that building a championship team required sustained effort and commitment.

Mental Toughness: The Kings cultivated mental toughness, which allowed them to stay focused and positive during difficult times. They kept their eyes on the prize, never losing sight of their goals.

Enduring the Grind: Basketball demanded rigorous training, continuous improvement, and hard work. The Kings embraced the grind, understanding that enduring the process was essential for achieving greatness.

Staying Committed: The Kings remained committed to their craft, putting in the time and effort needed to excel in every aspect of the game.

Pushing Beyond Limits: The Kings consistently pushed beyond their limits, setting higher standards for themselves and striving to reach new heights.

Overcoming Fatigue: Endurance allowed the Kings to overcome fatigue and keep performing at a high level, especially during intense games and challenging stretches in the season.

Perseverance Through Setbacks: The Kings faced setbacks, but they persevered with unwavering determination. They used setbacks as fuel for growth and improvement.

Weathering the Storm: The Kings remained steady during difficult times, knowing that storms were temporary and success awaited those who endured.

Celebrating Progress: Above all, the Kings celebrated every step of progress, recognizing that each milestone brought them closer to their ultimate goals.

As the East Texas Kings Basketball Program, LLC embraced the power of endurance, they knew that the heart of a champion was not just about talent and skill, but about the ability to persist and maintain their passion and determination throughout their journey. Their path to greatness was a testament to the transformative power of endurance, reminding them that true greatness was achieved not just through talent but through the relentless pursuit of excellence.

And so, with hearts full of gratitude, determination, and the spirit of endurance, the East Texas Kings Basketball Program, LLC continued to march forward, forever leaving their mark on the world, one inspired and empowered athlete at a time. For the heart of a champion knows that true greatness is not just about reaching the destination but about the enduring journey of growth, resilience, and the pursuit of excellence in every step they take.

From Underdogs To Champions

Chapter Fifty-One: Building Strong Foundations

The East Texas Kings Basketball Program, LLC understood that success was built on strong foundations. They recognized that establishing a solid base was crucial for sustainable growth and long-term achievements. They focused on building a strong foundation in various aspects of their organization.

Team Unity: The Kings fostered a strong sense of unity among their players. They emphasized the importance of teamwork and cooperation, knowing that a united team could achieve great things.

Coaching Excellence: The Kings invested in exceptional coaching staff, ensuring that their players received top-notch guidance and mentorship.

Player Development: The Kings prioritized player development, providing tailored training and support to nurture each athlete's unique talents and potential.

Youth Programs: The Kings established robust youth development programs, laying the groundwork for the future by nurturing young talents and instilling a love for the game.

Community Support: The Kings built a strong relationship with their community, garnering unwavering support and loyalty from fans and local businesses.

Financial Stability: The Kings focused on financial stability, making sound financial decisions to ensure the longevity of their organization.

Organizational Values: The Kings established clear organizational values, which guided their decisions, actions, and interactions with others.

Facilities and Resources: The Kings provided their players with state-of-the-art facilities and resources, enabling them to train and compete at their best.

Innovation and Adaptability: The Kings embraced innovation and adaptability, staying current with the latest trends and technologies in basketball and sports management.

Cultivating a Winning Culture: Above all, the Kings worked to cultivate a winning culture, where excellence was not just a goal but a way of life within their organization.

As the East Texas Kings Basketball Program, LLC focused on building strong foundations, they knew that the heart of a champion was not just about individual achievements but about the collective strength of their organization. Their journey was a testament to the transformative power of strong foundations, reminding them that true greatness was achieved not just through victories on the court but through the solid framework upon which they built their dreams.

And so, with hearts full of gratitude, determination, and the spirit of building strong foundations, the East Texas Kings Basketball Program, LLC continued to march forward, forever leaving their mark on the world, one inspired and empowered athlete at a time. For the heart of a champion knows that true greatness is not just about the accolades but about the legacy they build by laying strong foundations for the generations to come.

From Underdogs To Champions

Chapter Fifty-Two: The Beauty of Team Dynamics

Within the East Texas Kings Basketball Program, LLC, the beauty of team dynamics was evident in every aspect of their journey. They understood that success in basketball was not just about individual talents but about the collective synergy, camaraderie, and collaboration that came from a unified team.

Trust and Communication: The Kings fostered a culture of trust and open communication. Players felt comfortable expressing their ideas and concerns, fostering a strong sense of camaraderie.

Embracing Diversity: The Kings celebrated the diversity within their team. They recognized that different playing styles and backgrounds enriched their gameplay and contributed to their success.

Complementary Skills: The Kings focused on developing players' individual skills while also creating a cohesive unit with complementary abilities that complemented one another on the court.

Supportive Environment: The Kings built a supportive environment where players uplifted each other and celebrated each other's successes.

Shared Goals: The Kings aligned their goals, both individual and collective, to create a unified vision for success on and off the court.

Handling Conflicts: The Kings understood that conflicts were inevitable within any team. They prioritized resolving conflicts constructively, strengthening their bonds in the process.

Celebrating Team Wins: The Kings celebrated team victories with enthusiasm, recognizing that each success was a result of their collective effort.

Emotional Resilience: The Kings developed emotional resilience, supporting each other through wins and losses and learning from every experience.

Shared Leadership: The Kings embraced shared leadership, encouraging every player to take on leadership roles and contribute to the team's growth.

Building Lasting Bonds: Above all, the Kings cherished the bonds they built within their team. They knew that the beauty of team dynamics extended far beyond the basketball court.

As the East Texas Kings Basketball Program, LLC experienced the beauty of team dynamics, they knew that the heart of a champion was not just about individual accolades but about the magic that happened when they came together as one united force. Their journey was a testament to the transformative power of team dynamics, reminding them that true greatness was achieved not just through individual brilliance but through the beauty of working together in harmony.

And so, with hearts full of gratitude, determination, and the spirit of embracing the beauty of team dynamics, the East Texas Kings Basketball Program LLC continued to march forward, forever leaving their mark on the world, one inspired and empowered athlete at a time. For the heart of a champion knows that true greatness is not just about personal achievements but about the joy and beauty of teamwork, creating a bond that transcends the game and becomes a lifelong treasure for every player in their journey through life.

Chapter Fifty-Three: Learning from Legends

The East Texas Kings Basketball Program, LLC recognized the value of learning from basketball legends who came before them. They understood that the wisdom and experiences of those who had achieved greatness could provide valuable insights and inspiration for their own journey.

Studying Basketball History: The Kings delved into the history of basketball, studying the achievements and strategies of legendary players and teams.

Learning from Mentors: The Kings sought guidance from experienced coaches, former players, and basketball experts who could share their knowledge and expertise.

Embracing Role Models: The Kings celebrated basketball legends as role models. They looked up to their work ethic, dedication, and contributions to the sport.

Watching Old Games: The Kings watched footage of classic basketball games, analyzing the skills and tactics used by legends in action.

Implementing Timeless Techniques: The Kings integrated timeless basketball techniques and fundamentals passed down by legends into their own training and gameplay.

Embodying Sportsmanship: The Kings valued sportsmanship, inspired by the examples set by legendary players who displayed grace and respect on and off the court.

Learning from Failures: The Kings acknowledged that even legends faced failures in their careers. They understood that learning from mistakes was an essential part of the journey to greatness.

Emulating Leadership: The Kings embraced the leadership qualities displayed by legendary players, aiming to lead their team with the same passion and determination.

About the Author

Justiss Hill is the founder and Head Coach for the East Texas Kings Basketball Program, LLC.

As a young man that grew up in the foster care system, this 28-year-old from Naples, Texas has made amazing accomplishments, graduating from Northeast Texas Community College with his culinary arts certification, and proving that with determination you can succeed in spite of your hardships.

With this drive and will to help others, he was able to turn a struggling basketball team into a group of champions.

With help from adults who are able to see his vision, he continues to inspire and encourage others to go from underdogs to champions.

Team Roster

Derius
Jayden
Jarell
Kayden
Malachi
Ayrlic
Joe
Kendrick
Adrian
Zach
Jay
Jamarcus
Tyrone
Jeremiah
Chad
Chase
Carlton

From Underdogs To Champions

From Underdogs To Champions

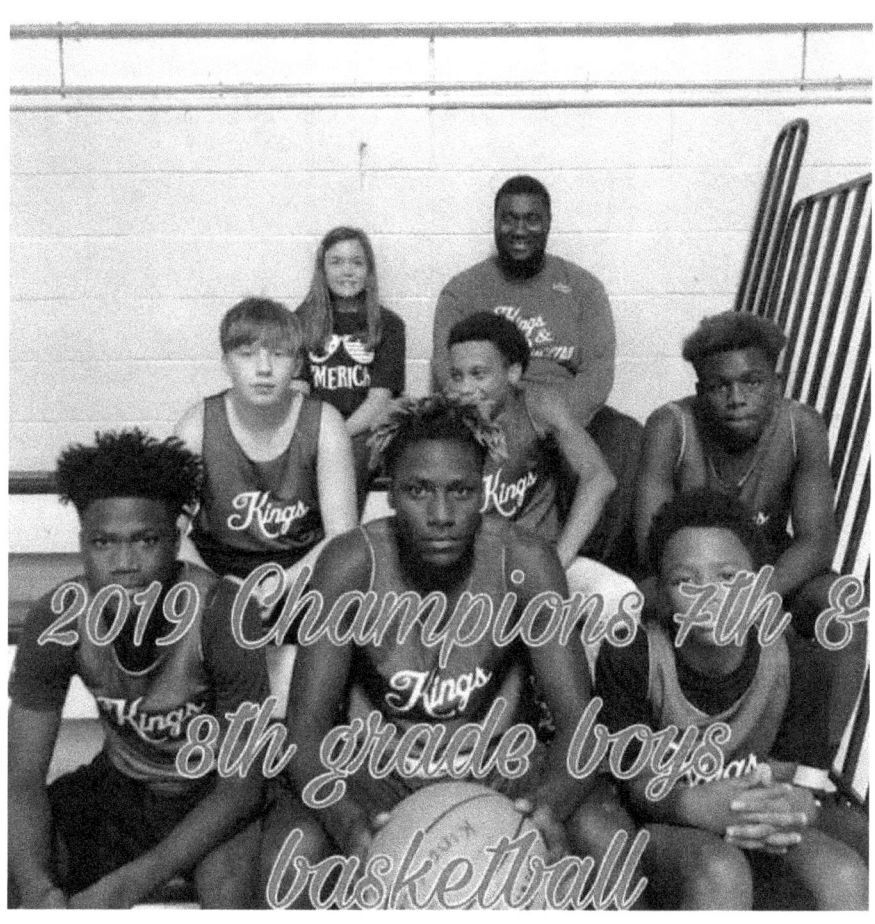

From Underdogs To Champions

From Underdogs To Champions

East Texas
KINGS

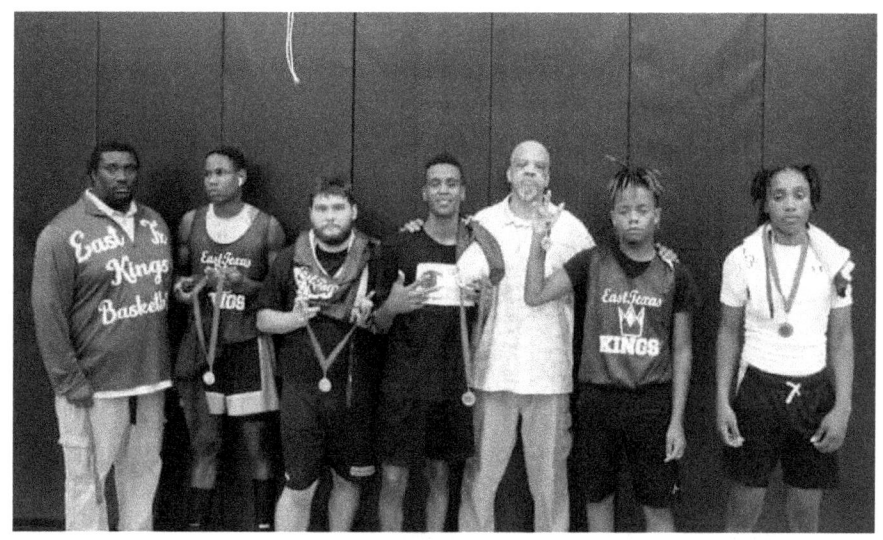

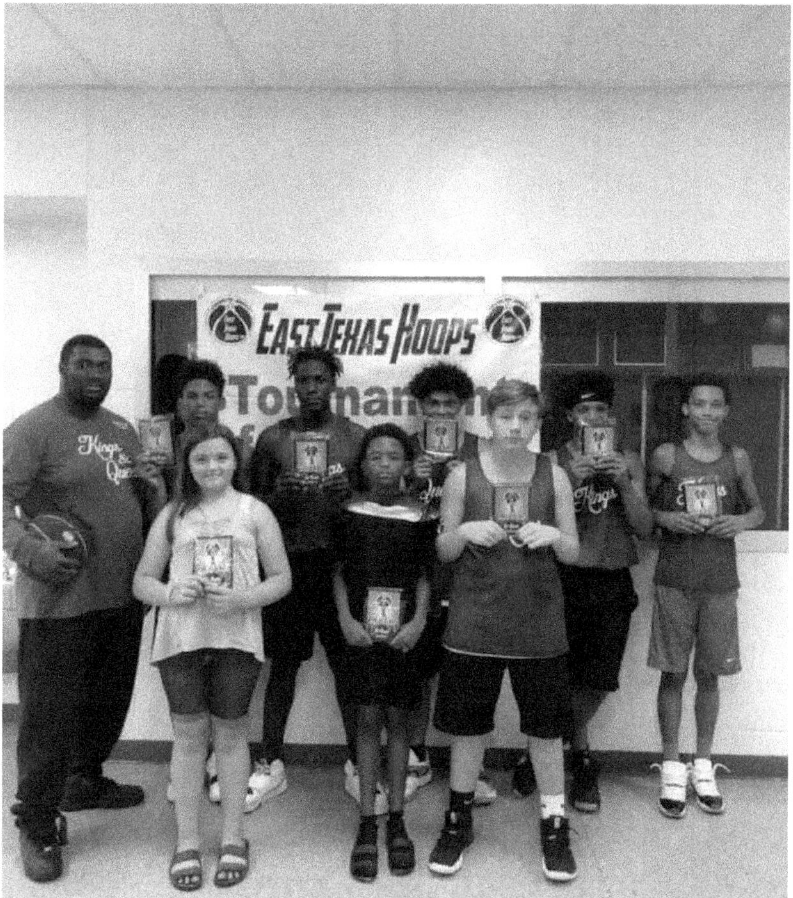
EAST TEXAS HOOPS

From Underdogs To Champions

Justiss Hill

From Underdogs To Champions

Douglas Reed was 16 years old when he passed on April 2, 2023.

www.ingramcontent.com/pod-product-compliance
Lightning Source LLC
Chambersburg PA
CBHW050900160426
43194CB00011B/2228